GROWER GUIDE No. 3

PEPPERS AND AUBERGINES

Denis Smith

GB

Grower Books · London

© Grower Books 1979
First published 1979

ISBN 0 901361 27 5

Designed and produced in Great Britain by
Sharp Print Management, Fakenham, Norfolk.

Contents

Introduction

Glasshouse vegetable growers have always shown interest in possible new crops. In some cases this interest may have been stimulated by the thought that a less demanding crop could be an easier alternative to modernisation. Recently, the increasing cost and decreasing availability of fuels has led to a search for other crops with a lower temperature response than, say, tomatoes or cucumbers. In neither case could peppers or aubergines claim to meet these requirements. Both are crops which demand a high temperature input to crop well, and both need to be grown in good glass with modern equipment to achieve their potential.

Nor could these crops be of value to the grower who lacks the skill to grow any of the more established crops profitably. It is a common fallacy that some crops 'grow themselves', as many have learned to their financial cost. Why, then, grow either peppers or aubergines, rather than a crop for which returns and profitability could be estimated with much more reliability?

There is certainly increasing demand for these crops in Western Europe. This is largely filled at present by imported field-grown crops, but there is no doubt that the market readily accepts the better quality product which the glasshouse grower can provide. And where there is a demand it is as certain in horticulture as in other industries that there will be someone to meet it. Flexibility has always been the key to success in growing, whether in techniques or in crops.

The level of knowledge of cultural aspects of growing both peppers and aubergines has been raised considerably in the last few years, largely by the enthusiasm of the Dutch horticultural industry and its technical back-up services. This publication attempts to bring together enough of the current knowledge of these crops to enable growers who would like to try one of these alternatives to do so with some hope of initial success.

Part I: Peppers

1:   Introduction; Equipment

The group of horticultural crops known collectively as capsicums, or peppers, are all members of the family Solanaceae, to which the tomato also belongs. Although the genus Capsicum consists of about thirty species, all but one of the commonly grown peppers are varieties of one species — Capsicum annuum — which originates in South America. While a few capsicums are grown for their decorative value, the majority of the varieties of commercial importance are edible. They generally have a hot taste, especially those with small fruit. The generic name comes from the Greek word 'kapto', meaning 'to bite', a reference to their pungency.

The larger-fruited varieties form the group known as the common capsicum, sweet, or red pepper. In fact, the fruit of this crop, which is the principal subject of this book, can be picked and marketed equally well either in a mature green state, or after it has ripened to red. (A number of recently-introduced varieties in fact ripen to a yellow colour). Smaller-fruited cultivated forms include the chillies, or the Bird Pepper, and the Bell Pepper. The chilli pepper is of economic importance, being used in the green state for pickling, or ripened and ground to form Cayenne pepper. The hot tabasco pepper, from Mexico, is different to the others in that it is a separate species, Capsicum frutescens.

Peppers are grown throughout the world, and enormous acreages are produced as field crops in many countries. However, this book will be concerned in particular with the culture of capsicums under protected cultivation, producing the high quality fruit which is demanded on the Western European market. Of course, many of the cultural aspects of pepper growing discussed will apply equally well to field crops, and can be adapted to a wide range of climatic situations.

The present consumption of green and red peppers in Europe is something of the order of 250 thousand tons per annum, of which about a quarter is produced in Europe under glass or polythene, while the rest is grown outdoors, mainly in Italy and other southern European areas, and to a lesser extent in Israel, North Africa and the USA.

The Netherlands are by far the largest Western European producers of peppers under glass, with a present area of about 500 acres, yielding 23,000 tons per annum. However, to put this in perspective, the Eastern European countries exported over ten thousand tons to the West in 1977. World trade in capsicums and related crops stood at about 75,000 tons in that year — but this excludes production for home consumption.

Peppers are grown in about ninety acres of glass in the UK at the present time. Although this area is four times what it was six or seven years ago, the production level of around seven thousand tons still only supplies a half of home consumption needs, the two main imports being from the Dutch and the Canary Islands.

Plant Structure and Habit

The pepper plant has woody stems and an upright habit. However, the stems are brittle, and tend to break or collapse when carrying a commercial weight of fruit. They therefore need a system of supports, alternative forms of which are discussed in Chapter Three.

The method of growth of the plant is shown in the diagram. The plant initially grows a single stem, but this soon branches into two. At the point of division there are produced one or more flower buds. The bud in the first branching position is known as the 'crown' bud. After the production of one or two more leaves, each branch subdivides once more, again developing flower buds at each point of division. These buds are referred to as the second layer flowers. Growth then continues in this way, although where no shoot removal is carried out many of the later side branches become very weak and fail to continue growth. This is the normal situation with net systems of crop supports.

With the stringing system of plant training described later, the required number of branches — usually one to four — are allowed to develop and then tied up. At each subsequent sub-division of these leaders, one of the two branches produced is twisted around the string to continue vertical development, while the other may either be stopped after one or two leaves or allowed to continue growth. This later growth, being unsupported, tends to collapse if fruit develops on it, giving the plant a more bushy appearance than more regular trimming out of sideshoots.

Flower buds develop at each level on the plant as described above. However, their ability to set and develop fruit depends on the vegetative strength and health of the plant. Under stress conditions the buds, especially any secondary buds which develop in addition to the primary bud at each point of division, will fail to open into flowers, but will turn yellow and drop off as they are rejected by the plant. The conditions required to encourage open flowers to set and develop fruit are described in a later chapter. Each fruit which sets successfully goes through an initial stage of rapid enlargement to its final size. This size will be largely governed by the vigour of the plant and the load of fruit which it is carrying.

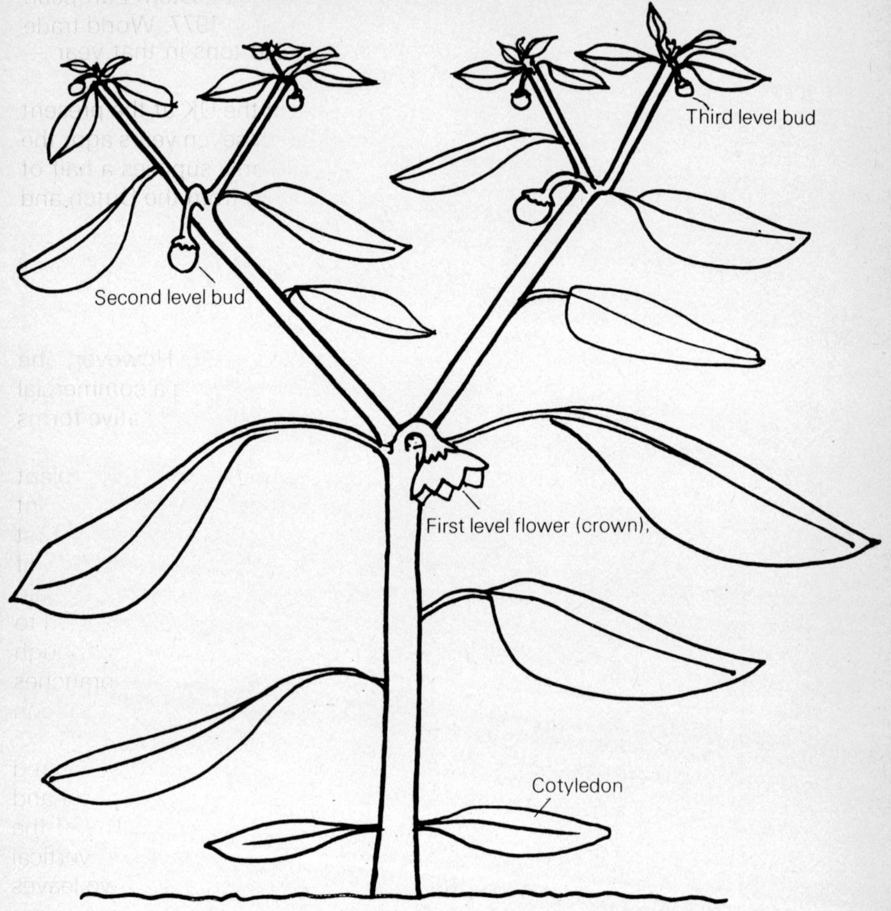

DIAGRAM 1:   Early growth of the pepper plant.

While it is developing, the surface of the fruit has a slightly wrinkled, matt appearance. The fruit should not be picked during this phase, because it loses water rapidly and softens. Once it gets to its final size the fruit becomes glossy, and is then described as having reached the 'mature green' stage. This is the normal and safe stage for picking green peppers. If the fruit is not picked at this stage, it will, after a period, begin to turn red. Since the colour turns in an irregular and patchy way, the fruit may not then be harvested until it has ripened fully to red.

Protected Cultivation

It has already been mentioned that peppers are grown as a field crop in many parts of the world, but that this book is orientated towards cultivation under the protection of glass or polythene, particularly in heated structures such as are needed for long-season production in Northwest Europe.

There are a wide range of structures under which peppers can be successfully grown, ranging from wide-span alloy glasshouses to polythene-covered tunnels of various widths. Generally speaking, any structure suitable for tomato or cucumber production is equally suitable for peppers. The one possible exception may be unheated and poorly ventilated plastic structures. Peppers are particularly susceptible to botrytis infection, and cultural methods of control by reduction of humidity are of considerable importance. Where the structure does not lend itself to this, the risks of botrytis becoming seriously established are much greater than with many other crops. Of course, there will be advantages and disadvantages in any particular type of house, both economic and cultural. The equipment needed for pepper growing is described in the following sections, and this, too, has to be taken into account when assessing the suitability of a particular nursery for this crop.

While it has been said that many structures are suitable for pepper growing, it must still be borne in mind that this crop, like many crops growing best under high temperature conditions, is very dependent on good winter light levels for satisfactory development. Because of this, the best early crops will be produced in structures with good light transmission, and older darker houses can be relied upon only to produce later spring or summer crops.

Heating Systems

The pepper plant is particularly sensitive to both air and substrate temperature, changes in vegetative vigour being rapidly translated into changes in yield. It is therefore necessary to consider the heating facilities as a primary factor when planning to grow early pepper crops. Although pepper crops can be successfully grown in unheated structures in some regions, they will be only short term crops, and their cropping season is limited to three or four months. Although precise temperature programmes for peppers have not been developed to the same extent as with tomatoes, the ability to provide adequate heating and ventilation, and to monitor and control the temperature, is indispensible for reliable programmed cropping.

The degree of heating capacity required for any particular crop will depend on the lowest anticipated outside temperature for the growing area, and to a lesser extent on prevailing wind speeds and on the airtightness of the structure. For example, the minimum ambient temperature in Southern

England in the winter months may be taken as −5°C. If it is intended to maintain a day air temperature of 20°C irrespective of weather conditions, then the heating system must be tailored to give a 25°C lift. In practice, it is probably adequate to accept, say, 15°C on the few occasions that the outside temperature is at its lowest, and plan for a 20°C lift.

The type of heating system installed will depend both on economics and on the capacity needed. The basic alternatives are piped hot water or steam, warm air, and undersoil heating. Undersoil heating is often combined with one of the other types of heating system as an additional facility. Warm air heating is the cheapest to install, but has cultural disadvantages over piped systems. Warm air units cannot provide a steady low heat output to give air movement and a buoyant atmosphere in mild, still weather, and also the radiant heat effect from the pipes is absent, so the plants tend to look as if they have grown colder than air temperature readings indicate. Warm air heating also has the disadvantage that horizontal temperature distribution, an important factor in any programme growing system, often becomes uneven in units of any size.

Conversely, though, warm air units have advantages over piped systems other than their low capital cost. They respond more rapidly to changing

FIG 1. Aubergines in a polythene tunnel. Both peppers and aubergines can be grown under polythene, but some form of heating is necessary to discourage high humidities, especially for aubergines. A pipe heating system is better than warm air.

conditions, and they provide more flexibility during crop turn-round, when the floor area of the structure can be left completely clear for mechanical cultivation and transport.

The ability to apply substrate heating to the pepper crops is of considerable value, as is discussed in Chapter Three. This can be done in a number of ways, depending on the growing system. With soil-planted crops it is usual to bury a loop of small-bore plastic pipe beneath each bed at a depth of about 45cm (18 ins). These pipes are fed with hot water to provide a steady heat input whenever necessary, and controlled to maintain temperatures at the root zone within the required range. Crops grown in peat can be warmed with pipe loops beneath modules, or within or beneath troughs. Rockwool systems have their own form of installation (see later), while Nutrient Film Technique units can apply heat directly to the circulating solution. With all these forms of substrate heating there is likely to be an economy of running costs, as the crop responds particularly well to increased root zone temperature, and will develop satisfactorily at lower air temperatures without loss of vigour or fruit setting.

Ventilation

There are two basic alternative systems for ventilating glasshouses or other structures. Natural ventilation depends on air exchange caused by wind or convection through gaps in the structure. Forced ventilation uses fans to provide positive air movement. Fan ventilation is more generally used for crops which have a considerable response to temperature reduction, and which therefore justify the high running costs. This is not a category in which pepper crops can generally be put, although there will be some growing areas where climatic conditions may warrant the installation of fan ventilation.

The position and size of ventilators will depend on climatic factors. Although pepper crops respond well to high temperature conditions, air temperatures in excess of 30°C will always reduce crop vigour, and should be avoided. In Western European growing conditions it is an accepted standard that the minimum ventilation openings provided in the structure should be equivalent to 15% of the floor area, but a greater ventilation facility than this is often an advantage, and so areas of 25% or more are commonly installed in modern structures.

Temperature Control

Heating and ventilation systems will need to be controlled from thermostats located within the growing area. These should be housed within a structure known as an aspirated screen, which can either be home-made or one of a number of alternative commercial designs. The principle is simple.

Thermostats, and recording equipment, are housed in a container which is shielded from the sun, and through which air is continually being drawn by means of a small electric fan. This set-up provides a much more accurate sampling of the air temperature than units which are not aspirated, however well they are shaded.

Control of heating systems is a complex subject best left to qualified engineers. Alternatives range from a simple on-off thermostat operating on a motorised valve on a piped system or directly on a warm air boiler unit, to complex two-stage electronic systems controlling heating and ventilation from a single sensor and costing several hundred pounds. The type of controlling equipment installed will depend on a number of factors — the time the grower himself is able to give to balancing the environment manually, the economics of the alternatives, and the availability of qualified servicing for the more complex installations. At the present state of knowledge of pepper growing, the plant's response to small changes in the temperature regime is not sufficiently well documented to warrant very fine control of the environment. If a combination of the grower and his equipment can control positive heating temperatures to within 1-2°C and ventilation temperatures to 4-5°C, then any further refinement is unlikely to be of cultural benefit.

FIG 2. Environmental control can be fully automated, with temperature levels adjusted according to light levels received by a solarimeter, but there is no evidence to confirm that such a set-up gives any crop advantage. Humidity control is probably a more important factor.

Thermal Screens and Double Glazing

Because the pepper crop requires such a high temperature regime, needing an even greater fuel input than a corresponding tomato crop, the possibility of installing thermal screens in modern structures capable of taking them comes to mind. The principle of thermal screens is that they cover the cropping area at night, reducing considerably the heat loss from the structure and so both saving the grower money (which nevertheless has to be set against the capital cost of the installation) and conserving fuel — an important factor in this energy-conscious world. During the day the screen is pulled back to allow more or less unrestricted light transmission.

Thermal screens undoubtedly save fuel, although their economic value is by no means as clear cut as was at one time imagined. What is not so well known at present is their effect on crops. Humidity levels are bound to be higher under some conditions, and this alone may preclude their use for peppers, adding to the potential risks of botrytis.

An alternative possibility for saving fuel comes in the form of double glazing. In northern Europe this is already being recommended as an economic investment, and there are also developments in the USA using double skinned polythene on its own or under a glazed structure. The problem with all these systems is that day-time light transmission is reduced, and the effect of this on cropping potential can be considerable. Again, the overall economics are by no means clear, and current thinking in some quarters is that double glazing and similar materials may be of value for incorporation in the sides and ends of the structure, but not for the roof. Of course, the picture will vary according to the growing region, because local light levels, ambient temperatures and wind speed will combine to give different results in different areas.

Temperature Recording

It is as important to be able to monitor air and soil temperatures as it is to be able to control them, and temperature recording facilities are therefore a necessary part of the equipment list for pepper growing. The first, and most fundamental, requirement is a simple mercury-in-glass air thermometer. This should be unmounted, so that it can be pushed into a propagation pot or into soil or peat in a growing system to indicate compost temperatures. Reading a thermometer in this way first thing in the morning, and again in the late afternoon, gives a fair indication of mean root temperature.

The same type of thermometer can be used to make up an integrating bottle to record mean night air temperatures. The bottle, filled with water, irons out short-term fluctuations in air temperature, and gives a good approximation to the average air temperature integrated over the previous two or three hours. It is not suitable for day temperature records, as it is affected by direct sun radiation, and for this reason must be read first thing in the morning before the sun hits the bottle.

Day air temperature is best noted by using a mercury thermometer suspended in the aspirated screen which houses the thermostats used for temperature control. To obtain a mean day temperature rather than instantaneous readings it is necessary to use a thermograph which provides a trace of temperature from which averages can be calculated. A thermograph would still need to be housed in an aspirated screen to reduce the effect of direct sun heat. To provide an approximate indication of general temperatures, but without the accuracy of a thermograph, a thermometer recording maximum and minimum temperatures can be used, but again needs to be housed in a properly-constructed screen to indicate meaningful day temperatures. A free-standing air thermometer, even in a shaded position, is not adequate.

Carbon Dioxide Equipment

All green plants need carbon dioxide (CO_2). By using the energy from sunlight, CO_2 is removed from the surrounding air and converted into plant material, sugars and other carbohydrates. This manufacturing process is called photosynthesis and can only occur during the hours of daylight or under extremely high levels of artificial light. Within limits, the higher the light intensity, the faster the rate of CO_2 assimilation. Higher temperatures also speed up the process. The natural atmosphere contains around 0.03% CO_2, often expressed as 300 parts per million (ppm) or volumes per million (vpm).

With the ventilators open CO_2 will be present at the normal 300 ppm with fresh air bringing in CO_2 as fast as the plants can assimilate it. With the ventilators closed, the CO_2 levels will fall during the day and may fall to a level which seriously retards plant growth. This is most likely to occur under sunny conditions where CO_2 is being used up more rapidly and if there is little wind to create air change through the laps, levels may fall as low at 125ppm. During the night, no CO_2 is used and the plants actually release CO_2 as a result of respiration. With the ventilators closed, levels of 400ppm may be reached by dawn. By raising the CO_2 level artificially (CO_2 enrichment) not only are low levels avoided, but also the plants show an increasing response as the level is raised above the normal 300ppm.

Extra CO_2 enables a plant to manufacture more carbohydrates than an unenriched plant, so that the time to reach maturity is shortened and a greater weight of plant material is produced. This is reflected in earlier bulking of crops together with a higher total yield. The maximum amount of CO_2 is utilised at high temperature and high light intensity, making enrichment particularly advantageous for crops such as peppers, which tolerate higher ventilation temperatures than many other crops.

Carbon dioxide can be supplied to glasshouses in a number of ways. Pure carbon dioxide can be injected into the houses from bulk storage tanks. Propane can be burned in small burners within the house. Paraffin of a suitable grade can be burned in a central unit and ducted to individual houses, or burned in smaller free-standing units within the structure. Waste exhaust gases from the heating system can be ducted to the houses where these are low enough in toxic by-products to be suitable for use. The last method is commonly used in Holland, where the natural gas used as a heating fuel is of a suitable standard.

The type of installation needed will depend on the materials available for carbon dioxide production. To get the best out of the installation, it is necessary also to have a time-clock so that enrichment can be applied at the right time, and if automatic ventilation is installed it is also necessary to have a cut-off switch to turn off the CO_2 producer when the ventilators are open.

Both paraffin and propane burning equipment should be positioned carefully to ensure that a free and uninterrupted supply of air is available for good clean combustion of the fuel. All intake openings must be free of obstructions and frequent inspections are necessary to make certain that wind-blown debris such as leaves, paper and thin polythene sheeting does not obstruct the air intake openings. Burners should be visited from time to time whilst they are operating to make certain that the equipment is functioning correctly. Paraffin burners can be heard from a distance when operating but a close inspection is required to see that the flame is lit and is burning correctly. Burners cannot be assumed to be working simply because the air intake fan can be heard running. Where duct openings, in separate houses or bays, are fitted with valves to control CO_2 distribution the valve settings should be noted and recorded so that if they are unintentionally disturbed through vibration or during maintenance work the original valve positions can be re-set easily and accurately.

The levels of enrichment needed and the times of application are considered in later chapters. Although the precise economics of carbon dioxide enrichment have not been as clearly established as with tomatoes, there is no doubt that both the cost of the installation and the running costs will be amply repaid in extra and earlier yield. Trials in Holland have indicated almost doubling the yield in the first two months of harvesting from CO_2 enrichment.

Irrigation Systems

Soil-grown peppers can be watered in a number of ways. On a small scale, hose watering is accurate and effective, but has largely been superceded by a range of automatic systems on commercial nurseries. Unlike tomatoes, peppers cannot safely be watered at any time during the season by overhead spraylines, because of their greater sensitivity to botrytis induced in high humidity conditions. There are, however, a number of suitable commercial low-level irrigation systems, including trickle or drip units, low-level sprinklers and spraylines, and lay-flat polythene tubing.

All such systems have their advantages and disadvantages, and some are cheaper to install or maintain than others. The most important factor which must be kept in mind is that a reasonably accurate volume of water should be applied where it is needed, and uniformly distributed throughout the crop, making allowance where necessary for areas which dry more rapidly than others.

For watering pepper crops in soilless substrates such as peat or rockwool, more precision is needed, especially in the case of low-volume isolated units such as peat modules or single-plant containers. In these situations, an accurate drip or trickle system is essential, protected from blockages by filters as necessary.

In association with any system of watering, there should be installed a suitable unit for applying liquid fertilisers. A number of alternatives are available, from expensive injection-type units, through various types and sizes of dilutor barrels, to the simple but reliable system of adding fertilisers directly to the reservoir or storage tank. The suitability of these alternatives may be limited to some extent by the irrigation system employed.

2: Plant Propagation

Choice of Variety

There are many commercial varieties of pepper available at the present time, and more varieties are being added to the list each year as seed producers improve their stocks to supply demand for both glasshouse and outdoor production.

The most popular varieties for glasshouse use in Holland are those based on the Sweet Westland stock. There are all varieties which bear thick-walled blocky fruit, and which have a high temperature requirement for optimum production. In the UK and Guernsey there is a preference for thinner-walled varieties such as New Ace. These produce fruit a little earlier, and can cope better with lower temperature regimes. Several varieties from the USA, where they are used for outdoor production, are also suitable for growing under glass in Europe. These include Bell Boy, Yolo Wonder and California Wonder. These varieties are high yielding, but not early.

Seed houses developing new varieties of pepper have to take into account a number of factors which will be of commercial importance apart from yield, including fruit shape, appearance, reliability to maintain shape, and thick walls for a longer shelf-life, especially in the red stage. Breeders generally also look for a degree of tolerance to Tobacco Mosaic Virus, and release only those varieties which show no reaction to inoculation by a mild strain of the virus. In recent years it has been shown that there is a significant demand for yellow peppers on the West European market, and so several breeders are now releasing varieties of this type.

There has also been a certain amount of interest in Holland in varieties which are self-stopping, and which require less training and trimming. Although varieties of this type are now available, they generally yield fruit which has a poorer shape and thinner wall than standard varieties. Their growing habit also makes them more susceptible to botrytis. In view of the range of varieties now available, growers are always advised to grow a few plants of new introductions among their standard variety, so that they can form their own opinions of the potential of such material under their own cultural programme.

FIG 3. Yellow-fruited peppers are meeting a good demand in Europe. Recent varieties give better quality fruit than this early introduction.

Seed Sowing and Germination

Pepper seed does not have a long shelf-life, and so only fresh seed produced the previous season should be used to be sure of a rapid and uniform emergence. The seed count is usually within the range 100-140 per gram (3000-4000 per ounce), so one gram of seed will generally raise about 80-100 plants for growing on.

Seed can be sown in either a soil-based or a soilless seedling compost of low nutritional status in boxes. The seed can be thinly scattered at a density of about 1000 per square metre (100 per square foot) or space-sown 2-3cm square. Space-sowing is an advantage if supplementary illumination is to be given (see below). Alternatively, seed may be sown individually into the containers to be used for propagation. This is an expensive method for winter production, because fuel costs during the period of germination and early growth are high, but may be more practical for spring and summer sowings, as the labour requirement for pricking off is eliminated, and plant development continues without a growth check.

On a large scale it is common to prepare an area of the glasshouse floor as a seed-bed, and to sow at a density of 1-2gm seed per square metre. The seed-bed can then be covered with a sheet of plastic film to maintain soil moisture and temperature, but care has to be taken that the soil temperature does not get too high during periods of bright sun.

Whatever system is used, the seed should be covered with soil or compost to a depth of about ½ cm, and this should be lightly firmed before watering gently with a fine spray. The surface should then be covered with plastic sheet, or glass and paper, until emergences begins, to retain moisture.

Peppers have a higher temperature requirement than tomatoes for successful germination. Current recommendations range from 21°-28°C (70-82°F), and the precise regime chosen will depend on economic and timing factors. Emergence will occur about one week earlier at 28°C than at 21°C. A suitable temperature for most conditions would be around 24°C (75°F) day and night until emergence, with perhaps rather higher temperatures when these are allowed to run up during sunny weather.

The Propagation Stage

Pepper seedlings will be ready to prick off after twelve to eighteen days, according to temperature. Two and a half weeks is the most common germination stage for winter-started crops, while seed sown in the late spring for autumn cropping will reach pricking-off size in about twelve days. The containers used for propagation can take a number of forms, as can the compost. Whatever system is employed, it must be remembered that the plant is usually held in the container for longer than tomatoes, and so the compost volume should be proportionally larger.

A plastic pot or a bituminised paper pot should have a diameter in the range 10-12cm, while soil blocks should have an equivalent volume. Pots will generally be filled with a suitable soilless compost with sufficient nutrients added to carry the plant through until liquid feeding commences — such as a standard proprietary peat propagation compost. Particular techniques such as growing in rockwool or nutrient film may require a different propagation procedure. This is considered under the appropriate headings.

The technique of pricking-off is the same as for tomatoes. The young plant should be eased out of the seedling compost, held by one of the seed leaves rather than by the stem, and inserted into a hole made in the propagation compost in such a way that the roots are allowed their full depth. Firming in should be just sufficient to fill up the air space around the roots with compost, and the seedling should then be watered in.

The pots should be placed in such a way that there are only small gaps between them at first, so that they do not dry out excessively, and then gradually spaced out so that the leaves never overlap. This means that a

FIG 4. Propagation conditions should encourage a warm rooting medium by allowing good air circulation around the pots. Slatted staging is better than solid benches or boxes from this point of view.

final spacing of 20 x·20cm may be needed, giving 25 plants per square metre. An even wider spacing, say 16 plants per square metre, may be used to delay moving the plants into the cropping house where this is convenient. The final density depends on how long the plants are held, the widest spacing allowing up to twelve weeks from sowing to standing out in the winter, but only eight weeks during summer plant raising.

Propagation Temperatures

Once seedlings have fully emerged, the air temperature can be allowed to drop a little. A temperature regime within the range 18-23°C (65-73°F) is suitable, according to light conditions, and day temperatures may be allowed to run up higher in sun, say to 25°C (77°F).

Pepper plants are very temperature-dependent, and good vigorous growth will only be achieved with a high temperature regime. Plants raised in low temperature conditions seldom develop sufficient vegetative growth to support a heavy crop. Of particular importance in this respect is the root temperature, and so it is generally better to propagate plants on benches rather than on the floor. The exception to this is of course where under-soil heating is available.

Benches should be constructed in such a way that the propagation compost remains as warm as possible in relation to the air temperature, and because of this it is particularly important to use slatted rather than solid staging. The additional temperature benefit to the pots from slatted benching can produce plants ready to stand out a week earlier than those raised on solid benches or in boxes. Ideally, the heat input to the propagation house should be from pipes situated under the benches to accentuate this effect.

Although raising atmospheric humidity around pepper crops by overhead spraying can be a dangerous technique because of the plant's proneness to botrytis, this problem does not generally occur during the propagation stage, as the plant is quickly dried by pipe heat. Because of this, it is possible to spray over the plants two or three times a day in sunny weather to maintain a buoyant atmosphere and encourage strong vegetative growth.

Artificial Lighting

The use of artificial lighting on vegetable plants during the propagation stage is of doubtful economic benefit in many situations. However, because the pepper plant remains compact, and so can be lit more economically than, say, tomatoes, and also because it is so light and temperature responsive, it may be worth considering the use of supplementary lighting for this crop.

Trials have been carried out on this technique. One such experiment in Guernsey used supplementary lighting from 400 watt mercury vapour lamps for a period of three to four weeks after pricking-off. The illumination period was for sixteen hours in every twenty four. The vegetative effect of lighting was quite pronounced, giving a ten day advantage in time to flowering from a mid-November sowing, and a fifteen day advantage from sowing in mid-December. In both cases, however, this advantage had been reduced to seven days by the time picking commenced. Whether artificial supplementary lighting is used in a commercial situation will therefore depend largely on the economics, particularly on the cost of electrical power.

Carbon Dioxide Enrichment

Enriching the atmosphere with carbon dioxide is a sound economic technique for peppers, even during the early stages of growth after pricking-off. The high temperature regimes employed for the crop can be used most effectively if carbon dioxide levels during the day are raised above ambient, and so enable growth during poor winter light conditions to remain strong. The equipment required and the alternative techniques available are described elsewhere, but it is particularly important to avoid levels of enrichment above 1000ppm during the propagation stage, as the tender young plants are very sensitive to accumulation of toxic by-products.

Watering and Feeding

The fine fibrous root system of the young pepper plant makes it particularly important that the compost should not be allowed to dry out excessively at any time during propagation, otherwise root damage will occur, and this will be reflected later in poor establishment after planting. Because of this, it is recommended that water should be applied little and often to maintain a fairly constant water balance in the pot. Conversely, the pot should not remain too wet for long periods, and so watering frequency may need to be reduced considerably in dull weather, especially in the early stages of propagation. The frequency of watering will of course depend very much on the weather and on growing conditions.

It is usual to apply a liquid feed with every watering once the plants have reached a particular stage of growth. This is defined as five to six weeks after pricking-off the seedlings in the winter, but may be as soon as four weeks in better light conditions. The feed used should be a medium potash feed incorporating phosphate, and can be made up by dissolving 680gms (1½lb) of potassium nitrate, 110gms (4oz) ammonium nitrate and 340gms (12oz) mon-ammonium phosphate in two hundred gallons of water (or in one gallon, and then diluting at 1 in 200, if a suitable system if available).

Fuel Economy

Since pepper plants grow relatively slowly in the poor light conditions of winter, there exists the possibility that plants could be held, for a period after propagation, in a smaller area of glasshouse than a faster-growing crop such as tomatoes.

A suitable system would be to stand the plants on 20cm pots once they reach the normal standing-out stage of growth, which are then held virtually pot thick in an area about a quarter size of the eventual planting area. Bud removal should be carried out as usual and planting into the pot done at the normal stage. The containers are then moved into their final growing positions when the flowers on the third level are about to open — this will be about a month after standing out.

The advantages of this system are that one month's fuel and carbon dioxide consumption is saved from three quarters of the production area, and that this area can be used to finish off any previous crop. Because of this fuel saving, it may be possible to run a higher temperature regime during this period than would be economical otherwise.

The principle disadvantage is the labour required to set out and move the pots, and also the materials cost involved. There is an additional problem of watering the containers while they are pot thick in the reduced area of glass.

To operate this system it is of course necessary to have a suitable isolated area of glass, but if this is available then the remainder of the growing area could be less well heated, as a temperature drop when fruit setting begins is culturally acceptable.

Planting Density

The most commonly-used planting density for glasshouse production is between 8,000 and 10,000 plants per acre (20,000-25,000 per hectare). The density is sometimes increased to about 11-12,000 plants per acre for short crops, particularly where the net system of supports is to be used. Trials in both Guernsey and Holland have demonstrated that wider spacings, as with tomatoes, do not necessarily result in lower yields, and can have advantages in terms of labour input and culture. For the vertical stringing system of training, as described in a later section, it is perhaps an advantage to plant up at twice the normal density, and train up two stems per plant rather than three or four. In this way the root system of each plant is supporting only half the crop weight at any one time, and plant vigour remains greater.

Plant lay-out depends on the lay-out of the structure and heating system, and on the training system adopted. In standard multi-span glasshouses, three rows of plants are grown per 3.20m bay, to give a density of 2 plants per square metre (8,000 plants per acre) by spacing at 50cm down the row.

Soil Preparation

The principles of soil preparation before planting peppers are much the same as for other vegetable crops. The soil should be clean of pest, disease and weed problems, and so will require steam or chemical sterilisation (see Chapter 6). If the previous crop was such that salt levels may have built up in the rooting zone, then the soil should be flooded prior to preparation to leach out excess nutrients and other salts. Soil analysis carried out at this time will indicate whether this is necessary, and will also give a guide to base dressing requirements. Water quantities needed for flooding will vary according to soil type, drainage, and the seriousness of the problem, but a normal rate may be taken to be between ten and thirty gallons per square metre, applied in up to four applications at about daily

FIG 5. Plants should be spaced out before leaves overlap. These plants are too large, with flowers open, and establishment after planting will be difficult. Flowers and buds will need to be removed to encourage vegetative growth.

intervals. If leaching is not necessary, then a light application of between five and ten gallons per square metre should be given two or three weeks before planting, and after initial cultivation, to bring the water content of the soil up to field capacity.

Initial cultivation involves breaking up any pan which may inhibit drainage, and incoporating such materials as peat or bulky manures to improve the structural condition of the soil. Final cultivations, carried out shortly before bringing in the plants, include incorporating any necessary lime and inorganic base fertilisers, and marking out and making paths, etc.

Base Fertilisers

Peppers must be given every encouragement to establish quickly into the border soil after planting, and to help this it is usual to start with lower nutrients in the soil than for tomatoes. Base dressing of suitable fertilisers should be planned to provide the following nutrient status at planting time: —

1. A soil pH of 6.0 to 6.5 (higher is suitable if unavoidable).

2. Sufficient phosphate for the entire season's growth.

3. High enough nitrate levels to encourage a good rate of vegetative growth.

4. Only sufficient potash for initial requirements — excess levels raise the salt content and inhibit rooting out of the pot.

The base fertiliser recommendations to achieve these aims will vary widely according to region and soil type, and should be based on soil analysis and local experience.

Stage of Planting

Peppers should generally be planted when the first ('crown') flower bud is visible. Plants held longer than this will establish less quickly, and vegetative growth may not be adequate to support an early crop. This means either resorting to extra flower bud removal , and so later picking, or accepting a greater reduction in plant vigour which will be difficult to recover at a later stage. In the better growing conditions which are usually met when late or autumn crops are being planted it is possible to plant at a slightly earlier stage, especially where high day temperatures may tend to reduce vegetative development.

3:   Growing On

The ability of a pepper plant to maintain its vigour over a long season's cropping depends to a large extent on rapid establishment into the growing-on house. There are a number of requirements for satisfactory establishment — a good, clean root system in the propagation pot, warm soil in good condition free from pests and diseases, and good climatic conditions after planting. It is usual to plant out peppers directly the crown bud can be seen in the head of the plants. The plant is still quite small at this time, and the root system should fill the propagation pot without being too restricted. Delaying planting beyond this stage can cause a reduction of vigour which will be difficult to recover later. It is particularly important to use a small plant when planting into less than optimum conditions, especially if the soil is colder than it should be. Conversely, if planting into a very good rooting medium, such as into a warm peat compost, the plants can be a little larger, but only if they are in pots large enough to prevent excessive root restriction.

Soil temperature must be high at planting time to encourage rapid rooting out of the propagation pot. The optimum soil temperatures are about 22-24°C (71-75°F), and every effort should be made to achieve these levels. The best early crops will be grown in structures with undersoil heating, and the cost of such an installation is generally accepted to be justified in terms of good establishment and early crop vigour. In the absence of undersoil heating, the planting date should be delayed according to the alternative heating system which is available. Pipe heating systems usually warm the soil better than warm air units, and so permit earlier crops to be grown. There are one or two techniques which can help raise soil temperatures to assist good rooting out, and these include raising the level of the soil in the trench by the addition of bulky soil conditioners, so that the sun can bring up the temperature during the day, and planting in large (20-24cm) containers to produce a similar effect.

As well as being warm, the soil or substrate should be in good physical condition. It should not be too wet, but should remain moist enough for good root action, and it should have a good structure so that there is good aeration. Peppers are particularly sensitive to high nutrient and salt levels in the soil, which inhibit root growth, and it is essential to leach out any excess nutrients before planting, preferably according to substrate analysis. The soil should, of course, be free of pest and disease problems, preferably having been effectively sterilised before planting. The planting depth should be quite shallow to discourage rhizoctonia attacking the base of the stem. This has the added advantage that the roots are then working closer to the surface of the soil in the earlier stages, where temperatures are usually higher and aeration and water content closer to optimum.

Flower Removal

Because of the importance of encouraging initial vegetative development, it is common practice to remove the flower buds from the first and second layers, so that fruit development does not check the plants before they build up sufficient growth to support a good crop. The need for this will depend on particular circumstances, as ideal conditions for establishment may make this technique unnecessary — in fact, very strong growth may cause the plant to abort its flowers naturally. An alternative method commonly used to prevent early fruit development from stunting growth after planting is to run high temperatures, particularly at night, for the first week or two. A regime of 20-21°C (68°F) at night and 24-25°C (75°F) during the day is generally enough to cause flowers to open small and then to abort rather than to develop fruit. The aim should be to clear flowers off from the first 40cm (16ins) of growth, but if it appears that the plant is not coming back into good flower production above this height a gradual reduction of night temperatures down to 16°C (61°F) over a period of a few days will soon bring a return to balanced growth.

Temperatures and Fruit Setting

For the production of a large well-shaped pepper it is necessary to encourage a good flower which will quickly develop a fruit. This in turn requires a strongly-growing plant, as weak vegetative growth results in the production of small blooms which either abort or develop slowly into small poor-shaped peppers. This balance between plant vigour and fruit development is controlled culturally by temperature, assuming that other cultural factors are all satisfactory.

As has already been mentioned, high temperatures after planting encourage strong vegetative growth at the expense of flower development and fruit setting. Once a good root action has been established and shoot growth has reach about 40cm (16ins) from the ground, temperatures should be reduced to restore the balance. A normal regime for this stage would be 18-19°C (65°F) at night 22-23°C (72°F) by day, and ventilating at

FIG 6. Optimum cultural conditions for pepper culture under glass have been examined at Experimental Stations both in Holland and in the UK. This work, combined with growers' experience, forms the basis of current recommendations.

27°C (80°F). If flower size is slow to recover, then the night temperature can be further lowered to 16°C (61°F), but gradually over three or four nights. The maximum rate of fruit development will occur with a night temperature of 15-17°C, but a regime as low as this should be used only with caution, because of the risk of overloading the plant with fruit and so stunting the crop for future production. In poorly heated structures, where temperatures may be rather lower than this on occasions, growth will be slow, and a heavy flush of fruit initially will be followed by a period of vegetative recovery during which little fruit will be produced. The crop is very dependent on high temperatures for satisfactory growth, and night temperatures as low as 10-12°C (50-54°F) are sufficient to almost completely inhibit growth.

A strongly-growing crop can cope well with day temperatures as high as 30°C (86°F) in sun, but temperatures of 35°C (95°F) and above are harmful, and should be avoided. Humidity levels should be kept quite high in good weather, perhaps around 75% RH, by spraying over as necessary. Too dry an atmosphere in otherwise good growing conditions is likely to cause flower abortion. Conversely, excessive overhead damping down of the crop should be avoided, especially late in the day, because of the crop's susceptibility to botrytis. Water quality should be checked, because overhead spraying with water of poor quality, particularly if the sodium or chloride level is high, is likely to produce a marginal scorch on the leaves. To encourage drying out of the crop in a period of high atmospheric humidity it is important to be able to apply heat below the crop to encourage air movement, which in turn reduces the risk of the foliage and fruit becoming wet. For this purpose, a pipe heating system is of greater value than warm air heating, and should be used with a little ventilation where necessary.

Watering and Feeding

Because of the need to maintain a good level of vegetative growth in peppers, the watering programme is of some importance. The root system of the pepper plant, although strong, is sensitive to damage by either drying out or waterlogging, and this rapidly reduces plant vigour. The frequency and quantity of water application cannot be standardised, because both will vary widely with, for example, the climate, the vigour of the plants, and the soil structure. As a general rule, the soil should be brought up to field capacity with each application of water, and should be allowed to dry back a little before the next application. In this way the roots are encouraged to search for water and so develop more extensively, and can then cope better with any stress conditions which the plants may meet subsequently. Drying back to the point at which the plants flag will cause root scorch, and this may be followed by infection of fungal root rots. If drying back of the soil reaches this stage it is particularly important to allow the plants to recover with a small application of clear water before applying any liquid feed. Excessive variation in the water content of the substrate also encourages fruit cracking, and induces 'black spot' on the fruit if the salt level in the soil is at all high.

Watering should generally be on a 'little and often' basis during the period of establishment following planting, and then greater quantities given as plant vigour develops. Once picking begins it is usual to reduce watering a little, and it is especially important to do so when the heating system is turned off, as water consumption usually falls dramatically for a week or two at this time. Generally, greater quantities of water are needed where a soil warming system is in use than when air heating alone is employed.

Although peppers do not require such a high nutrient level as tomatoes, it is still preferable to apply liquid feed at each watering. This can be a medium potash (1.0.2) formula, although to encourage vegetative growth it may be necessary to use a medium nitrogen (1.0.1) feed for a period. On lighter soils, a medium nitrogen feed may be used continuously to maintain nitrogen levels. The feed strength should generally be lower than for tomatoes, aiming for a potash level of 200-300ppm in the feed, according to the type used. Formulae for making up and diluting stocks of suitable feeds are given in an appendix.

Training the Plants

There are two basic alternatives for training and trimming pepper plants. Either the plants can be grown up strings, and a limited number of leaders taken per plant, or the plants can be supported by horizontal nets, when all shoots are usually left unstopped. The yield potential from either system appears to be much the same.

With the stringing method it is common to take three or four leaders per plant, and to stop all sideshoots beyond the first or second leaf. It is also possible to use a double planting density and to take only two leaders per plant. In this way the plant growth and yield may be marginally improved, although the cost of plants will be higher. Using this method the stem is usually twisted every two or three weeks through the season. Stopping the sideshoots may be done as often as weekly or as seldom as monthly. It has been suggested that a monthly schedule has no adverse effect on

FIG 7. Planting arrangement will depend on the layout of the growing house, and final shoot density determined by the plant spacing in the row and the number of shoots tied up per plant.

FIG 8. Good extension growth on the shoots being tied up indicates satisfactory plant establishment in the trench. Early flowers have been removed, and flowers now opening will be allowed to develop fruit.

production. Although the crop becomes leafier and picking rather slower, there is a labour saving of up to ten per cent compared with more frequent trimming.

The alternative training system, supporting unstopped plants with horizontal nets, requires more labour at the start, but less during the cropping period, when an occasional tucking-in of plants is all that is needed. Nets of a mesh size of about 20cm are suitable, and should run every 30cm or so, the lowest being 50-60cm above the floor. Wires and cross-strings can be used instead of wire nets, giving a saving in materials costs at the expense of a higher labour requirement.

Although the net system of training appears more attractive in terms of mid-season trimming labour input, there are disadvantages which make it generally less satisfactory than vertical training. Picking is very much slower, and more damage is done to the plants in the course of finding the fruit. Because of this, and because the foliage density is greater, the risk of botrytis is greatly increased, especially in structures where high humidities are often encountered. Finally, crop clearance at the end of the season takes much longer with crops which have been netted rather than trained.

Carbon Dioxide Enrichment

Carbon dioxide enrichment should be applied at the level of 1,000ppm from dawn to dusk throughout the season until the frequency of ventilation is such that this is no longer justified. If a fuel such as propane or paraffin is

FIG 9. Strong vegetative growth encourages large flowers and rapid fruit development. This ensures a good yield and well-shaped fruit.

being burned for this purpose, it is usual to run this equipment from dawn for eight hours per day, and to assume that an input of sixty pounds of CO_2 per acre per hour will provide a suitable level of enrichment.

Higher than recommended levels of enrichment carry increased risks of toxic by-products of combustion damaging the crop, as also can faulty combustion. Ethylene, carbon monoxide, and oxides of nitrogen and sulphur, can all cause visible symptoms on the crop — leaf scorches and drooping, and bud abortion — and can also inhibit photosynthesis and growth without visible symptoms in some situations. Pollution problems are generally more severe during calm, dull conditions, and most likely to occur in light, tightly-glazed modern glasshouses.

To avoid the risk of crop damage by pollutants when using carbon dioxide equipment it is important to service burners regularly, and to ensure that excessively high levels of carbon dioxide enrichment are not maintained. During calm weather it is a worthwhile precaution to ventilate for 15-30 minutes in the middle of the afternoon to purge the atmosphere.

In long houses, particularly those built on a slope, a problem of inadequate distribution of CO_2 can arise. Local temperature effects may accentuate problems of uneven distribution, and if differences in growth are observed, CO_2 levels should be checked and additional inputs or ducting provided as necessary.

Harvesting: Picking Stage

Growers who are not accustomed to peppers are often uncertain as to the

FIG 10. A strongly-growing leader will develop fruit on side-breaks as well as in the leaf axils on the main stem. If vigour is maintained the plant will be able to support good fruit development and still continue extension growth.

correct stage at which to pick the fruit. There is, however, a particular point at which a fruit reaches what is described as the 'mature green' stage. The fruit surface changes from a matt, wrinkled appearance to become darker green and glossy. Peppers harvested before this stage do not hold or travel well, and quickly soften, and so it is important that this change is recognised. With experience, it soon becomes a matter of habit to pick green fruit at the right time.

If fruit is left on the plant beyond the mature green stage it will eventually turn red. Once this change has started, the fruit has to remain on the plant until it has reached a uniform red colour. This will take up to six weeks after the mature green stage. The arguments for and against allowing the fruit to develop to the red stage are covered below.

The most common method of harvesting peppers is to break the fruit away from the plant by hand. There is a natural fracture line where the peduncle, or stalk, joins the stem, and it is important that the peduncle remains attached to the fruit after harvesting. Some growers use a knife, scissors or secateurs to harvest peppers, and these may be more or less successful according to the habit of the crop. Whatever method is used to pick, care must be taken to avoid breaking stems, as this provides an ideal site for the establishment of botrytis in the crop. For this reason it is often better not to pick early in the morning, as the plants are at their most brittle at this time, and damage is most likely to be caused.

The standard for picking frequency has in the past been once a week, even during the summer months. This is adequate from the point of view of fruit quality, since a mature green fruit will remain unchanged on the plant for a week or more before starting to turn red in parts. However, it is likely that plants picked over more frequently — even twice per week — produce larger fruit, and therefore heavier crops. This is because a mature fruit remaining on the plant longer than necessary will help to overload the plant, and so retard further fruit development. Labour studies suggest that total harvesting effort is not significantly greater if the crop is picked over more or less frequently, as the time needed per box of fruit remains fairly constant.

Picking Stage — Red or Green?

The question of whether to allow a proportion of the crop to develop red fruit, and at what stage of the crop this should be done, is always a problem for the grower. Certainly, the returns for red peppers can be very attractive, especially in the early part of the season when the amount of red fruit on the market is low and demand is correspondingly high.

There are several factors which must be taken into account. The crop must be sufficiently developed to withstand the strain of carrying red fruit, which must remain on the plant for three to six weeks past the mature green stage. Growth must be vigorous to enable flowers to continue setting despite this extra load on the plant. As already mentioned, the health and vigour of the crop determines the amount of fruit it can support, and once this level is reached other flowers will abort.

A reduction in yield must be expected where crops are allowed to develop red fruit. For example, crops harvested red from late May onwards from a well-growing crop would yield only 75—80% of the crop which would have been picked as mature green fruit. Of course, this yield loss must be offset against the additional market value for red fruit. This premium may vary widely through the season, according to the situation of supply and demand in the markets.

In commercial practice, many growers start by allowing a small proportion of fruit to turn red, while continuing to pick the majority green. The proportion of red to green can increase as the plants become larger and stronger. To make picking easier, a part of the total area can be used solely to produce red fruit. It must be remembered, though, that a proportion of the crop will at some stage be out of production for a month, often when green fruit would be fetching a reasonable return. There is no guarantee

FIG 11. Dense foliage makes picking more difficult, and this may cause stems to be broken and disease to become established in the crop. Net-supported crops are more susceptible to this problem than tied crops, where fruit access is better even at high stem densities.

that the red fruit will fetch the anticipated premium when it is finally picked.

At certain times in the summer months a change may be worthwhile in the system of picking. For example, if there is a continued period of low prices for green fruit, then a greater proportion can be left to turn. This avoids the expense of harvesting and marketing fruit in a period of low returns. However, the problem here is that other growers will be doing the same, and so the red fruit is equally likely to fall into a low price period when it in turn is picked.

Fruit Grading

The grading standard and system used must obviously depend on the requirements of the market to which the fruit is to be sent. There are three aspects of grading which may have to be considered; colour, size and quality. Colour grading is simple. Most markets require a separation of green and red fruit, although a mixed pack may be acceptable in some situations. A partly-red fruit is taken as a quality fault, and is marketable only in the lowest grade, if at all.

Size grading may be necessary for some markets. A suitable series of grades would be 55-65mm diameter, 65-75mm, and over 75mm. Alternatively, size may be one aspect of quality grading, where first grade fruit may need to be 60mm or larger.

Quality grading is always important to achieve a good market reputation, and the criteria recommended for export of peppers from Guernsey provide a suitable basis. There are a series of general minimum quality requirements, and the specific requirements for two quality grades.

The capsicums must be: —

whole;
sound;
clean;
free of foreign smell or taste;
well developed;
free of damage caused by frost;
free of unhealed injuries;
free from sunburns (except as specified for Class II)
fresh in appearance; and,
of such state as to allow the capsicums to withstand transport and handling and to ensure arrival of the produce at market in good condition.

Class I

Capsicums in this class must be: —

of good quality;
firm;
of shape, degree of development and colour normal for the variety;
with the peduncle attached, cut not less than one centimetere from the calyx;
virtually free of blemish;
This class may be exported either at *green* or *red* stage of ripeness.
Minimum size (diameter at widest point) 60mm.

Class II

This class includes capsicums which cannot be graded in Class I but which meet the minimum requirements defined above.

They may have defects as follows, provided these do not seriously detract from their appearance: —

defects of shape and development;
sunburns or minor injuries not more than 1cm^2 per capsicum, or 2cm long in the case of elongated injuries;
small dry surface cracks not exceeding cumulative 3cm in length;
less firmness without being withered;
slightly damaged peduncle, provided it is cut no less than 1cm from the calyx.

This class may be exported either at *green* or *red* stages of ripeness, and additional as a *'mixed'* pack.
Minimum size (diameter at widest point) 50mm.

Packing and Marketing

There are a number of containers suitable for transporting and marketing peppers, ranging from open returnable wooden crates for local marketing to disposable cardboard boxes with lids for long distance shipment. Generally, much the same form of packing is needed as for tomatoes. Small units are most suitable, and the four or five kilogram box is the standard in Western Europe. Provided they are picked mature, peppers travel well, and have a long shelf life. Transportation generally presents no problems although the containers must of course be strong enough to prevent physical damage, and also large enough to take the required weight of fruit without squashing. Ventilation should be provided to prevent excessive build-up of humidity in the container, with the consequent risk of development of incipient botrytis lesions.

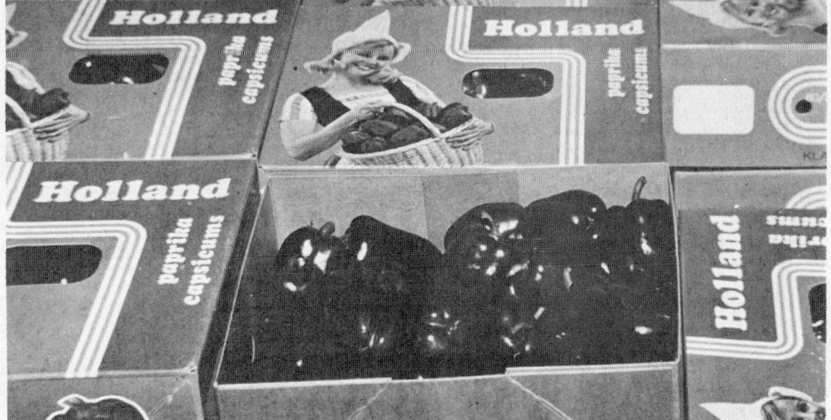

FIG 12. Peppers should be packed for transport in strong containers with sufficient volume to avoid the risk of crushing the fruit during shipment. As with all products, attractive packaging and clear labelling help to achieve a good price.

4:   Growing Systems

Peat Culture Systems

A number of artificial media developed and used commercially for tomatoes and cucumbers have been successfully adapted to growing peppers. Of these, the techniques for peat culture have been most fully established.

The main reasons for changing from soil to peat are: —

(a) Problems with poorly drained soils or from persistent soil borne pests and diseases.

(b) The high cost of steam or chemical sterilisation.

(c) A faster turn-round at the end of a crop allowing an extended picking season.

In addition, it has been found that the picking date is advanced because of the rapid establishment and growth of crops in peat, leading to an increase in early yield.

Sphagnum moss peats are most commonly used but Sedge peats and 'younger' less-humified Sphagnum moss peat are also available to the grower. Lime and nutrients should be mixed into the peat before use according to the formula given in the appendix. All types of peat substrates should give similar results but management techniques, particularly in watering, have to be altered due to different water holding characteristics between peats. Becauses of this, it is important that only one type of peat is used on an irrigation system. It is equally important that the selected peat is uniform in its physical characteristics. Uneven drying out can lead to serious management problems.

Many methods of growing in peat have been successfully demonstrated, but the two methods most commonly used are peat modules and troughs. Growing in three plant modules has proved the most popular system in Guernsey, allowing ½ cubic foot (14 litres) of peat per plant. Paths are raised by about 5cm to confine surplus water to the trenches. Trenches should be raked to ensure all the modules will lie in an identical fashion.

Polythene should be laid to cover the whole floor. Modules are then spaced out according to the plant spacing required, with stitched ends (if present) all facing the same way for even drainage.

All the peat should be moistened before planting. One way to achieve this is to fill the modules with water by irrigation equipment before standing out; allow twenty-four hours for the peat to absorb all the water it can hold and slit the modules to release surplus water. Drainage slits should be cut at the ends or on one side of the modules, 3cm above ground level.

A number of trough installations are available commercially, or can be constructed from readily available materials, using the same or more peat per plant as is used in modules. Growers have sometimes found it difficult to achieve the same yields in peat troughs compared to modules. One reason for this may be the higher levels of total soluble salts that can occur through continual evaporation of water from the surface of the peat. Covering the trough surface with polythene or occasional hose watering should prevent high soluble salt levels occurring. A further difficulty with troughs can arise in cleaning the houses thoroughly at the end of the season to ensure that persistent diseases do not carry over to the next season.

Culture in Peat

Growing in peat is straightforward provided that management techniques are correct and certain essentials are attended to.

Ensure that the peat is properly moist before planting.

Planting should not normally take place before the stage described for soil growing. Plants establish very quickly in peat and an excessively vegtative plant could be produced from planting at an earlier stage.

Setting the base of the propagating pot 2-3cm deep in the peat provides adequate stability. Leaving the pot on the surface of the peat can damage the young roots when the pots rock during handling of the plants. Planting deeply in modules, or attempting to moisten dry peat after roots have grown to the bottom of the module, can lead to root rotting or root death from waterlogged conditions.

Watering and Feeding in Peat

Watering is the most critical technique to master in peat growing. An accurate system of drip irrigation is essential for peat modules. A regular programme of watering should be established to keep the peat reasonably moist at all times. The following points should be noted for watering crops in peat substrates: —

(1) A drained trough or module is essential.

(2) Extra drips should be provided for fronts and hot gable ends.

FIG 13. Wet foliage, especially late in the day, is dangerous, as high humidity increases the risk of botrytis, to which both pepper and aubergine crops are very susceptible. Because of this, overhead watering or spraying must be carried out only with caution, when conditions are suitable.

(3)   The amount of water applied should be directly related to the light received and the rate of crop development.

(4)   When the daily water requirement exceeds 1,500 gallons per acre the amount should be split into morning and afternoon applications.

(5)   The plants will need up to 50% less water during the two week period after heating is turned off, at the end of June or early July.

An accurate system of applying dilute liquid fertilisers is necessary. Basically, crop feeding is similar in free draining peat systems and in soil. The major difference is the inclusion of phosphate, as this is readily leached from the peat. This can be supplied as medium potash containing phosphate, and should be fed an average of once for every three feeds without phosphate (see appendix). Calcium feeds should rarely be necessary and should never be mixed with phosphate as the fertilisers do not mix and will be rendered insoluble.

Trace elements may be added to the feed occasionally, using a total chelated trace element mixture. Regular peat samples for analysis should be taken from planting, and then monthly, to check the levels of nutrients in the peat. The reliability of an analysis depends upon how well the sample represents the area from which it is taken. Correct sampling is essential to avoid misleading analytical figures.

Growing in Rockwool

Rockwool is an artificial growing medium made from a mixture of basalt and limestone. It is available in the form of slabs, designed to hold about 60% water and 40% air, and is a suitable inert substrate for a number of commercial crops, including peppers. About 100 acres of crops in Holland and the UK are at present grown in rockwool, and the area is increasing annually as cultural expertise becomes greater. Rockwool growing appears to have many of the advantages of NFT systems, but without the problems involved with a re-circulating solution.

The usual set-up is to propagate plants in small cubes of rockwool draped in black plastic film. Nutrition and watering have to be quite precise during the propagation phase. The Dutch recommend rainwater for the best results, and a liquid feed containing nitrate, phosphate, potash, calcium, magnesium, and trace elements should be used. The blocks must be placed, separated, on an even surface, to avoid them remaining too wet in dull weather. Propagation systems using other substrates do not appear to establish as well on to rockwool at planting time.

At planting time the rockwool cubes are placed on to the main slabs of rockwool in the growing house, and allowed to root in. They are given liquid feed with every watering as for peat systems, using trickle or drip irrigation, but in the case of rockwool it is also necessary to include trace elements. The rockwool bed must be even to allow uniform watering, and a big advantage with this system is that warm water can be circulated through plastic pipes set into the under side of the rockwool slab to provide substrate warming. It is probable that a better spread of warmth is achieved from the pipes into the rockwool if they are set into grooves in a base sheet of polystyrene, which then also acts as a level base for the rockwool slabs (see diagram).

Nutrient Film Technique

A natural step beyond rockwool growing is to do away with the inert rooting media altogether, and to grow the crop with its roots bare, and bathed in a circulating solution of nutrients. This system, known as nutrient film technique (NFT), is developing rapidly in both technology and application at the present time, and is a particular system of the method of

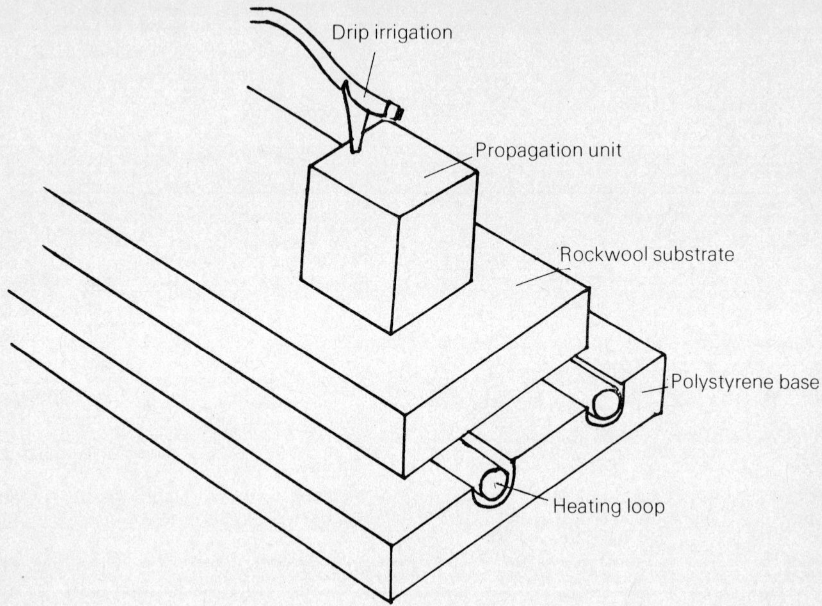

DIAGRAM 2:   A Rockwool growing system.

growing known as hydroponics, or hydro-culture, which has been around for many years in many forms.

As its name implies, nutrient film systems are based on a very shallow stream of water flowing over the roots of the plants, and which contains dissolved in it all the nutrients needed for plant growth. The solution depth must be minimal, because the mat of roots which the plants develop must sit partly in the air space above the solution circulating in its gully. In this way the plants can continuously take up both water and oxygen in balanced proportions, giving them an advantage over plants grown in the soil, where there must always be a fluctuating compromise between air and water.

NFT systems are being employed commercially on a wide range of crops in many countries now. A great deal of fundamental work has been carried out at the Glasshouse Crops Research Institute in England, and their efforts, backed by a number of enthusiastic growers, have resulted in a reliable technique for the commercial production of glasshouse vegetable crops, particularly tomatoes and cucumbers. Small-scale trials with peppers suggest that this crop, too, would adapt well to NFT, just as it already has to growing in peat and rockwool. The root system of peppers is strong and extensive, and the ability to apply differential air and soil temperatures just by heating or cooling the circulating nutrient solution lends itself to the cultural requirements of peppers.

FIGS 14. & 15. The young plants on the left (Fig 14) have been inoculated with virus, and show considerable stunting and leaf distortion compared with the healthy seedlings of the same age on the right (Fig 15).

The advantages of NFT methods compared with soil or peat growing are centred on the ability to provide precisely monitored and controlled environmental conditions — water availability, nutrient balance and salt content, and temperature at the roots. Although the capital cost of a fully automated system is high this can be compensated in a number of ways. There is no need to provide a separate irrigation system, and there will also be savings in water usage, which will be particularly important in some situations, giving a strong financial argument in favour of NFT in developing countries with arid climates.

There is a considerable potential for fuel saving where heating is required for economic crop production, particularly where high root temperatures can provide balanced vegetative growth under conditions of low air temperatures — a situation which may be well suited to peppers. Other advantages of NFT are related to crop management, especially to crop turn-round time. Peat and rockwool systems reduce this unproductive phase of growing by avoiding or speeding up substrate sterilisation between crops. NFT goes one stage further, by eliminating all carting out of material other than of the old crop itself, and a turn-round time of five days under commercial conditions is quite feasible.

There are, of course, disadvantages to nutrient film growing, too. Apart from the initial capital cost there is the problem of providing management experience in what has become a rather sophisticated growing system.

There are a number of cultural problems which can develop without warning, and which need immediate corrective action if disaster is to be avoided. There is no buffering action of a substrate to prevent sudden changes in nutrient availability, and so imbalances and deficiencies can occur quickly and with serious consequences. The root system can die back over a period of a few days, and can require considerable cultural expertise to encourage it to recover to an active state. There is also the potential risk of diseases spreading unchecked in the circulating nutrient solution, and so moving throughout the entire system in a matter of hours, although this disadvantage may be offset by the ability to circulate systemic pesticides in the solution itself.

There is no doubt that peppers could be grown successfully in an NFT system, given our present state of knowledge of the technique, although the uncertainties are still such that the wise grower, however enthusiastic, would treat NFT initially as an experimental system rather than as a reliable commercial proposition. It is possible to buy made-to-measure 'kits' for NFT growing, and this form of installation will obviously appeal more to the grower with no practical experience of nutrient film growing than will developing his own system.

There is a lot of information readily available on this system of growing, and this information is as important to successful NFT growing as the installation itself. Recent publications cover many aspects of nutrient film growing, and provide a sound basis of facts for any one intending to grown crops with this technique.

5:   Programmes; Cost and Returns

The following notes give an indication of suitable programmes for early, late and autumn crops, together with a note of limitations in terms of equipment, and any cultural points which are particularly relevant.

Early Programme

For early pepper production it is necessary to sow seed between mid October and mid November. The propagation period will take eleven to twelve weeks, so that planting out date will be during January. Light levels and temperature are generaally higher during the early part of this propagation period, and so the number of weeks from sowing to planting will be less for the earliest sowings than for the later ones.

To achieve satisfactory establishment of crops planted in January requires the best facilities. The glass should be modern, because light transmission is especially important at this time of the year. There should be a pipe heating system, either steam or hot water, laid out through the crop and close to the ground to maintain good soil temperatures. Perimeter or overhead pipes are not suitable. Undersoil heating is ideal, and almost an essential for early crops grown in the Northern Europe. Growing conditions should be good — the soil structure should be open and free-draining, and the nutrient status low to encourage rapid rooting out into the trench. Peat and other soilless substrates are very suitable for early growing, as they can provide a warm rooting medium with optimum nutrient conditions, and there is little risk of root rot diseases becoming established on the developing rooting system of the plant.

The advantages of early production are two-fold. Firstly, the crop bulks up well in the period up to the end of May, and therefore commands good prices — there is a generally falling price pattern from March through to the summer months in both the UK and continental Europe, and so shifting the pattern of production forward a few weeks, provided the later cropping potential is not reduced, gives a good increase in market returns. The other advantage is in the length of the cropping period itself. A well-grown pepper crop will yield almost in proportion to the length of time it is in production, so high yields, in the order of 60-80 tons per acre or more, are more likely to be achieved with an early start.

There are, of course, disadvantages to early pepper production, too. Apart from the requirement of good glass and equipment, heating costs are proportionally higher than for later crops, especially as the highest temperature regime has to be run at the time of year when ambient temperatures are lowest. Carbon dioxide enrichment, which is an essential for early growing, may be more costly than for later sowings. The cultural difficulties of early production are also greater. Good establishment in the poor climatic conditions of January and February requires cultural expertise, as does maintaining a satisfactory balance between vegetative growth and fruit development during the early spring months.

Later Growing

Satisfactory crops of peppers can be grown from sowings made in December for planting out during February. With a later programme such as this, older houses with poorer light transmission may be acceptable, but soil temperature remains important, even though undersoil or substrate heating is no longer essential. Warm air heating does not allow such early plantings as piped systems, since soil temperatures are not raised to the same extent, and so growing houses with such installations should not generally be planted until March onwards, depending on the climate.

Later crops have the disadvantage that they come into full production after the high pepper prices of March and April are past, but, grown well, they can give a good total yield for the season, and continue producing into the autumn months when an improvement in market returns is usual. One obvious advantage, apart from the suitability of later programmes for less modern units, is in the lower fuel requirement. A crop planted out in mid March may need only a half of the fuel input of one started at the end of January. Carbon dioxide enrichment costs are also lower. (This technique is still worthwhile for later sowings and the increased returns should still cover the cost of enrichment and show some extra profit).

Culturally, there are advantages in later pepper production. Rapidly increasing light and temperature levels encourage good plant vigour and fruit development, and ability to apply full ventilation during sunny days reduces the risk of botrytis becoming established in the crop. This risk is much greater in earlier crops, where plant growth is slow, and ventilation is likely to be given less freely in dull, humid weather. Because of this, fuel costs for the earliest crops tend to be higher than predicted for providing the required temperature regime, because extra pipe heat often has to be applied with a little ventilation to encourage air movement to dry out the crop. It is usual to plant at rather high densities for short term crops, but this should not be done when it is intended to continue cropping into the late autumn.

Although the fuel requirements for later production are lower than for the earliest crops, they are still appreciable, and it may not be an economic proposition to grow peppers in unheated structures. In cold glasshouses with good ventilation it is possible to plant out peppers during April and May, but successful establishment is very much in the hands of the weather and the grower's ability to provide a good soil temperature. Even then, returns depend on market values during a short cropping period centred on July and August, when prices are usually at their lowest. As a general rule, the longer the growing season, then the heavier the total crop, even though the rapid growth and fruit development of summer-started crops gives a rather heavier production level initially.

Autumn Cropping

Growing peppers for autumn production is becoming increasingly popular, and rising prices towards the end of the year make it an economically attractive proposition to follow, say, early tomatoes or a flower crop. However, there are limitations to this programme of production which must be kept in mind. Although the crop can establish rapidly into the warm soil of the growing house when it is planted out in the summer, and early culture is simple, it is important to be able to maintain good clean growth well into the autumn, since it is in October and November that the largest part of the crop returns is produced. This means in particular being able to apply heat and ventilation to keep the crop dry during the period when botrytis becomes an increasing danger. This in turn means that only modern structures with a well laid out pipe heating system are suitable for autumn production, and also that fuel consumption for the cultural control of botrytis will represent a significant part of the total costs of the crop.

For autumn production it is necessary to sow only about six or seven weeks before the planting out date, as early plant growth during the propagation stage is fast. A wider plant spacing should be allowed than for earlier crops, as plant vigour is generally good following rapid establishment into the warm soil, and also because a lower plant or shoot density helps maintain a clean crop during the later stages of growth.

Labour Requirements

It is not possible to give precise labour requirements for pepper growing, as this will depend to a large extent on cropping programme and on the training method adopted. However, some general indications can be given. The labour input for cultural routine operations such as planting, tying, trimming and clearing the crop is probably a little lower than for tomatoes. If a low-labour system of growing is employed, for instance, by leaving sideshoots on the leaders unstopped, then the labour requirement during the growing season may be as low as a half of that needed to maintain a tomato crop. It is not clear at this stage whether crops grown to high or low labour inputs have the economic advantage, although there is a suggestion from management studies in Holland that growers who trim less frequently do not appear to lose out on production, provided the standard of work and culture is otherwise high. Overall, in the Netherlands, pepper growers appear to staff up to about 80-85% of the level tomato growers. .

Picking times will vary widely according to whether the crop is being picked green or red, whether the plant is open-trimmed or bushy, and on the frequency of harvesting. Similarly grading and packing rates will depend on the degree of automation, on the scale of the operation and on the form of presentation required by the market. Because of this only a very general estimate can be given. To pick green fruit on a weekly system and hand grade into 4 kg. boxes will take about 5-6 minutes per box, so that a crop of 80 tons per acre would have a picking and packing labour requirement of 25-30 man-hours per acre per week during the main production period.

Fuel Consumption

It will be realised from earlier discussion of temperature programmes that peppers are a crop with a high fuel requirement, both to maintain adequate growth and to provide suitable conditions for disease control. The actual fuel input will depend both on the growing programme adopted and on the climate. The following table gives an indication of likely fuel requirements for crops grown in the south coast of England or in Guernsey. Crops grown in more Nothern areas will need more. The figures are based on the assumption that the crop is grown in a good, multi-span glasshouse with an efficient heating system and a sheltered site. Consumption is quoted in units of 1000 litres per acre per month, using 200 second oil. Adjustments for differing situations may vary the figures given by as much as 25% either way, so they can only be used as a guide.

On the basis of these figures, an early heated tomato crop would have an annual fuel usage of about 150-170,000 litres per acre. This comparison may enable growers with knowledge of tomato fuel requirements on their nursery or in their growing region to extrapolate to give a more accurate indication of requirements for peppers.

To calculate an example based on a crop planted out at the beginning of February, and run at temperatures of 21°C night, 24°C day during the first month, then at 16°C night, 20°C day during March, rising again to 18°C

Night temp (°C)	14	16	17	16	18	17	18	21	21
Day temp (°C)	18	18	18	20	18	20	20	21	24
January	25	26	29	28	32	30	32	39	41
February	26	28	29	29	32	30	33	39	41
March	25	26	28	29	30	30	32	38	41
April	22	22	23	25	26	26	28	33	36
May	16	17	17	20	19	20	22	26	30
June	10	10	12	15	13	15	16	20	24
July	4	6	7	9	7	10	10	15	19
August	3	4	6	7	7	7	9	15	18
September	4	6	7	9	9	9	11	16	19
October	10	12	13	13	16	16	17	23	25
November	17	19	22	22	25	23	25	32	34
December	22	23	26	25	29	28	29	36	38

FUEL USAGE IN UNITS OF 1000 LITRES/ACRE

night, 20°C subsequently, and terminating at the end of September, the fuel requirement per acre would be as follows:

February	41,000	litres
March	29,000	,,
April	28,000	,,
May	22,000	,,
June	16,000	,,
July	10,000	,,
August	9,000	,,
September	11,000	,,
TOTAL	166,000	litres per acre

This figure does not include plant raising, and is on a par with tomato requirements only because the pepper crop in this instance is not planted until February, while a corresponding tomato crop would have been using fuel since late December.

Crop Costs

It is obviously impossible to quote reliable up-to-date costs of pepper production, since costs vary widely between growing areas, and also month by month within any particular area. Instead, it is proposed to give an example of costings for an early long-season pepper crop grown in Guernsey (at 1979 prices). From this, growers will be able to modify the headings according to their own situation and growing programme, and then apply current prices and values to this.

This example is based on a growing unit of $\frac{1}{10}$ acre.

Direct Costs	£
Plant raising	180
Soil sterilisation	210
Fuel	1,220
Paraffin for CO_2	200
Labour (incl. packing)	1,100
Fertilisers, pesticides	130
Sundries	80
Services (water, electric)	80
	£3,200

Overheads	
Rent or depreciation	600
Rates, taxes, repairs, etc.	300
	£4,100

To set against these costs it is necessary to make an estimate of returns. This is equally difficult, both from the point of view of yield pattern and from the value per box. As a rough guide, the following returns are based on pepper values on the UK markets in 1978:

Yield	*Net returns per $\frac{1}{10}$ acre*
60 tons per acre	£3,860
70 ,, ,, ,,	£4,508
80 ,, ,, ,,	£5,795
100 ,, ,, ,,	£6,440

Based on these figures, it is clear that the profitability of pepper growing is largely dependent on a good crop, and that yields well above 60 tons per acre are needed even to cover costs. The economics of later crops and crops grown for autumn production are less well established. Fuel costs will be lower, but so will yield, and the benefit of the high prices of March and April will be lost.

6: Pest and Disease Control

There are a large number of pests and several diseases which can attack pepper crops. Some of these, such as whitefly and botrytis, will already be well-known to most growers. Others, such as aphids and sclerotinia, are a less serious problem on most other glasshouse vegetable crops than they are on peppers.

As a general rule, sterilisation of the substrate and the glasshouse before introducing the crop is essential to reliable pest and disease control, as is sensible hygiene during the growing season. Sections on steam and chemical sterilisation at the end of the chapter cover the basic requirements for the provision of a clean rooting medium.

A further essential is good growing conditions with a high standard of culture. A weak or weakened plant is always the most susceptible to attack by pests or diseases. Similarly a poorly trimmed, dense crop is most likely to be infected with botrytis. Poor soil structure, poor drainage, poor ventilation and poor temperature control all create conditions more favourable for pests and diseases than for the crop. These factors cannot be stressed too strongly; all the fungicides and insecticides in the world will not overcome deficiencies in steriliation, hygiene or culture.

Control measures on peppers are generally the same as for other crops. However, it is preferable to apply pesticides for control problems on the aerial part of the plants as smoke or fog formulations, rather than as wet sprays. Although this is more expensive, it is also more effective, as the dense foliage of a well-grown pepper crop, especially trained in nets rather than on strings, is too dense for reliable coverage with a contact wet spray.

Red Spider Mite

The symptoms of red spider mite damage on peppers are much the same as on other glasshouse crops. Small yellow-white spots develop on the leaves, turning darker yellow eventually. The mites themselves can be seen on the underside of the leaves, either with the naked eye or with a hand lens. Plants frequently become infested early in the season, often during propagation, by adult female mites which have overwintered in the structure of the glasshouse or in equipment which has remained in the house and has not been sterilised. In severe attacks of red spider mite they form webs over the plants, particularly over the young shoots, in which many mites collect and later disperse to attack new growth.

Red spider mites develop and spread very quickly under high temperature conditions, and so pepper crops are particularly susceptible. They also prefer a dry atmosphere, so the reduction in overhead sprays recommended as a general rule to protect peppers from botrytis attack also favours the spread of spider mite. It is suggested that young plants, especially in weather conditions which do not encourage botrytis, should be damped down as often as possible where mites appear to be established in the crop.

Biological control of red spider mites on peppers is possible, using the predator Phytoseiulus persimilis, but has to be integrated with biological control of other pests, especially whitefly, as the range of pesticides which can be used on the crop without damage to the predator is limited (see section on whitefly on aubergines). Where chemical control of red spider mite is necessary, a number of acaricides can be used including quinomethionate smokes or wet spray, cyhexatin wet spray, and dicofol plus tetradifon, either as a wet spray or through a fogging machine. A soil application of oxamyl will also give control in the early stages before picking, where its use is permitted. It is now well known that strains of mites resistant to many pesticides are commonly encountered, particularly in intensive glasshouse areas. Where a pesticide does not appear to be giving control, an alternative, preferably from an unrelated chemical group, should be used.

Whitefly

The glasshouse whitefly, Trialeurodes vaporariorum, is a very common pest of horticultural crops, and pepper crops are no exception. As with red spider mite, the pest develops and multiplies much more rapidly in high temperature conditions, and can quickly reach epidemic proportions on peppers, causing extensive sooty mould which both marks the fruit and inhibits vegetative growth.

Some strains of whitefly are resistant to certain insecticides, and so chemicals should be alternated. Since most chemicals control only some stages of the life cycle of the whitefly, it is important to apply a sequence of three or four applications, four to seven days apart according to the temperature regime in use, to provide adequate control. Biological control, using the parasitic wasp Encarsia formosa, has been used successfully (see section on whitefly on aubergines).

Suitable insecticides for whitefly control on peppers include resmethrin, permethrin, diclorvos and malathion. As with other pests, smoke and fog formulations are preferable to high volume wet sprays.

Aphids

Peppers are very susceptible to attack by a number of species of aphids. They are easy to control chemically, because under glasshouse conditions they reproduce viviparously — the females produce live young rather than eggs — and so all stages of their life cycle are killed by aphicides. However, if control measures are not taken as soon as the problem is seen, leaves and fruit quickly become marked with sooty mould, and extension growth reduces as much of the effective leaf area of the plant is spoiled. Also, aphids are able to transmit and spread a number of the virus diseases which can attack peppers, and must therefore be dealt with as a matter of urgency. A number of aphicides are available, notably pirimicarb, and in all cases success depends on the ability to reach all pockets of aphids in the crop, so that smoke and fog applications are preferred to wet sprays.

Other Pests

Caterpillars occasionally cause some leaf damage in pepper crops, and can best be controlled with the bacterial suspension of Bacillus thuringiensis, marketed under a range of trade names. This has to be applied as a high volume spray, and so it is important to achieve a good coverage.

The feeding tunnels of leaf miners are sometimes seen on the lower leaves of peppers. These can be controlled by repeated applications of synthetic pyrethroids or nicotine, and the life cycle broken by means of a soil application of a suitable insecticide to prevent pupation of the larvae. Oxamyl or parathion will achieve this objective. Other insect pests sometimes noted on the foliage of peppers include earwigs, thrips, and begonia mites. These are generally susceptible to the chemicals suggested for the more common pests listed above.

There are also one or two pests which attack the root system of peppers below ground level, particularly millipedes and eelworm. Either of these problems can be controlled with a soil application of oxamyl, or alternatively by a soil drench with parathion, subject to the use of these materials being permitted.

Botrytis

Of the various diseases which can infect peppers, the most commonly encountered is undoubtedly grey mould, or botrytis. The common name comes from the light grey furry mould which forms on botrytis lesions in some conditions, and by which it is most easily identified. Botrytis is a disease which spreads by aerial spores, which germinate and develop only in humid conditions. When such conditions persist, as they can easily do under the dense foliage of a well-grown pepper crop, then the disease can

FIG 16. Caterpillar damage to pepper foliage. Although not often a serious problem, caterpillars can sometimes be difficult to control successfully, and so damage can become quite extensive on occasions.

FIG 17. Botrytis may attack stem, leaf or fruit, but causes most damage when it infects the stem, as it will generally spread until it causes the stem to collapse and die. In this case, botrytis has infected a snag left by clumsy harvesting.

spread quickly and with disastrous effects. Botrytis can affect individual fruit, and render them unmarketable, but the greatest problem is the stem lesions, which girdle the stem and cause it to die. The cropping potential can be seriously reduced in this way.

Because of the way in which botrytis becomes established and spreads in a pepper crop, the primary control measures are cultural. The crop should be well supported, and well trimmed, and air movement maintained through the foliage by whatever means are available. This can most reliably be achieved by introducing pipe heat below the crop, and ventilating as necessary to encourage circulation of warm air throught the canopy. Botrytis becomes established most easily on damaged plant material, and for this reason care should be taken in working the crop, especially during harvesting. Snags and broken leaves should be cut out and the crop kept clean and open at all times.

A number of fungicides are suitable for control of botrytis, but should be considered as a secondary line of defence behind cultural control measures.

Any of the benzimidazoles or dichlofluanid may be tried, preferably in low-volume applications, but some resistance may be found to some of these materials in some growing areas, and so chemicals should be alternated. Tecnazene or dicloran smokes may also be considered.

Sclerotinia

Sclerotinia is a fungus which attacks peppers in a rather similar way to botrytis. The lateral stems of the plant may show dark lesions, on which may develop a white fur under moist conditions. When the stem is broken through the internal tissue is brown. Like botrytis, sclerotinia spreads under moist conditions, and so the recommendations for the cultural control of botrytis apply equally to this disease. Chemical control mesures are the same as for botrytis. In the case of sclerotinia, diseased plant material should be put into polythene bags and removed from the house — stems allowed to fall to the floor and rot will provide a source of infection the following season.

Root Rots

Like all horticultural crops, peppers can be attacked by a number of root rot fungi, such as pythium and rhizoctonia, which can reduce the active root area of the plant and so reduce cropping potential. Root rots are generally secondary to cultural problems such as poor soil condition, waterlogging or physical scorches following fertiliser applications on to dry roots, etc. If the soil has been properly sterilised before planting, then root rot diseases are much less likely to become established, but attention must still be paid to good cultural conditions in the rooting zone. Root rots can be controlled chemically by such fungicides as zineb and copper-based materials, applied as soil drenches to permeate throughout the substrate to full root depth.

Virus

Peppers are subject to attack by a number of viruses, particularly tobacco mosaic virus (TMV) and Cucumber Virus 1. There is no chemical control for virus infection, and the answer lies primarily in the hands of the plant breeders. Recently introduced varieties generally have a good level of tolerance to TMV, but Cucumber Virus 1 is still a problem. Plants showing severe stunting and distortion which can be attributed to virus attack should be removed, and aphid control should be maintained, as this pest is probably the main agent of spread within a crop.

Soil Sterilisation — Steaming

Steam sterilisation of the soil (or of peat) is a standard technique for pest, disease and weed control for a wide range of horticultural crops, the following notes apply to all general situations, both for peppers and for aubergines. The object of steam sterilisation is to destroy selectively the harmful organisms in the soil, i.e. the disease organisms and pests (fungi, virus, bacteria, eelworms, and symphilids), whilst having the minimum adverse effect on beneficial organisms, and soil nutrients and structure. A temperature of 60°C (140°F) is sufficient to destroy most of the harmful pests and diseases, but not enought to inactivate virus particles. Virus inactivation is a time/temperature relationship, for instance a temperature of 80°C (180°F) for 15 minutes is sufficient and as the temperature increases the time is reduced.

Preparation of the Soil for Steaming: Steam will not readily penetrate hard soil or large lumps, and the soil should be broken up to a fairly fine tilth before steaming. Lumps of up to 5cm diameter will reach sterilisation temperature during steaming except if they are on the surface. With every lumpy soil there is a risk of 'blowing', resulting in inefficient steaming and a considerable loss of steam. If the soil is very wet at the time of steaming the steam will condense quickly, causing an increase in the moisture content and 'boiling'. The cost of steaming is also increased, as a large quantity of steam is used in raising the temperature of the water already in the soil.

Methods of Steaming:

(a)   Grid Steaming: This method consists of burying forked grids in the greenhouse trenches. The grids should be buried at two-thirds of steaming depth, that is at 30cm for steaming 45cm of loose soil, with soil broken up beneath the grids. For steaming 60cm deep, grids should be buried 40cm down.

(b)   Hoddesdon Pipes: These are single pipes as distinct from forked grids. Their function is similar to grids and they are buried to the same depth as a grid would be. The pipes are normally about 2 metres long, 3-4cm internal diameter, and having holes of 3mm diameter in pairs toward the underside of the pipes at 12cm intervals. The pipes are spaced 30-40cm apart but the spacing should not be more than 25% greater than the depth to which they are buried.

Hoddesdon pipes are useful when the whole floor is steamed in houses where there are few obstructions, e.g. large wide-span houses with small bore piping, and where large mechanised cultivations are used to prepare the soil for steaming.

(c)   Combs: These consist of a horizontal 4cm diameter pipe with downward pointing spikes or hollow tubes 20-30cm long and closed at the bottom with a solid point. Just behind the point, the tube is restricted or 'waisted' and through this waist, holes are drilled to allow the steam to escape into the soil. The horizontal tube is fitted with wooden handles, one at each end for long two-man combs, or a pair in the centre for one-man combs. Alternatively metal hooks may be used for lifting the hot combs.

The soil should be well broken up with a rotovator before steaming with the combs.

The combs are pushed into the soil to their full depth. The rate of steaming should be the same as that recommended for grids.

The trenches should be covered with PVC or canvas covers. While floor steaming these covers should be walked on when moving the combs to avoid stepping on the steamed soil.

(d) Pans or Tins; Flash Steaming: The soil should be thoroughly cultivated, but not broken up to finely, as the steam has to penetrate from the surface downwards and very fine soil restricts the movement of steam.

The depth of steaming with tins is limited as the pressure needed to overcome the resistance to the downward movement of steam is greater than that normally employed. This means that although the top 25-30cm is well steamed, the soil below that depth remains unsterilised, unless steaming is continued for a considerable length of time.

(e) Tile Drains: Permanent underground steaming mains of tile drains enable steaming to be carried out conveniently and quickly. The capital costs of this system are comparatively high, but the labour costs are low. In the future it may be possible to use plastic pipes with holes drilled at suitable intervals instead of tile drains.

The tile drains are buried 40cm deep and either one per trench or one per double trench, with a layer of coarse siftings spread the width of the trench surrounding and covering the land drain. The coarse siftings should be covered with finer siftings to seal the surface and prevent soil blocking the system. Care should be taken when cultivating to avoid dislodging the tile drains.

T-Piece steam injectors should be inserted at intervals so that 8-10m of trench is steamed either side of the point of injection. Check the temperature of the soil with a thermometer and put covers on when the steam is up all over. Where troughs are steamed in two sections a removable baffle must be placed in the drain to confine the steam to the section being steamed. These baffles should be removed after steaming if the tiles are expected to serve as drains, or if they will interfere with cultivations.

(f) Tunnel Steaming: With this system, the procedure is to cultivate the trenches thoroughly prior to making a pair of tunnels in each trench with a mole-type plough. Steam is injected from short open-ended grids inserted in the tunnels at approximately 4m intervals. The number of tunnels steamed will depend upon the capacity of the boiler.

Except when steam is applied from the top, as with the tin steaming or flash steaming methods, the surface of the soil will be both the last to heat up and the first to cool. It is, therefore, necessary to cover the soil with PVC or some other similar material, once the steam has reached the surface, to ensure that the steam is spread. At this stage the steam flow should be reduced by valving down just allowing sufficient steam to pass to keep the soil temperature at 99°C (210°F) at the surface. This will avoid filling the greenhouse with wasted steam, and will of course reduce the fuel consumption.

When peat is to be used as a soil conditioner it may be spread as a layer over the surface of the soil before steaming. This will serve as an insulation and will retain heat in the soil, ensuring that any lumps near the surface are more likely to be cooked. Covers should still be used in conjunction with the peat as the latter will not spread the steam.

Chemical Soil Sterilisation

There are two groups of chemicals used in soil sterilisation: —

(i)   General Sterilants, which have a wide spectrum of control, that is, they control eelworms, fungi, insects and weeds.

(ii)   Specific Sterilants, which control only one of the above organisms, generally only eelworms.

The following list covers most of the chemicals in common use under glass.

(a)   Cresylic Acid: Cresylic acid is a contact sterilant with a limited control range. It is used mainly as a surface sterilant in washing down the greenhouse structure and the soil surface following steam sterilisation.

(b)   Formaldehyde: Formaldehyde is widely used as a contact steriliant. It is a contact weed killer and fungicide but is not effective against eelworms or insects. This chemical is also used as a washing down and soil surface sterilant.

(c)   Metham Sodium: This is either a contact or fumigant sterilant, and has a wide spectrum of activity. It breaks down in the soil to a chemical called Methyl Iso-thiocyanate (MIC). MIC is the active principle and is absorbed onto the soil mositure which surrounds the soil particles. Application of metham sodium should be made in early autumn and not later than mid November. The time that elapses between application and safe planting is variable and depends on soil temperatures, soil moisture and soil type. In general, low temperatures, wet and highly organic soils give slow release of the chemical.

(d)   Methyl Iso-thio-cyanide (MIC):   This chemical contains the same active principle as metham sodium. It therefore has very similar properties.

(e)   Dazomet: Dazomet is a chemical supplied in powder form that also breaks down to MIC, the formulation making it better to handle. Application is more difficult and involves a precise operation. The powder is

FIG 18. Sun scald on a pepper fruit. This is often a problem with fruit exposed directly to the sun under high temperature conditions. This crop has been marked with a high volume fungicide spray, and the fruit will need to be wiped clean before it is marketed.

spread evenly over the soil surface and then rotovated into the soil.

(f)   Chloropicrin: This is a specific fumigant. It is a fungicide that has proved useful against wilt diseases and root rots. The chemical is injected into the soil and the soil surface sealed. Chloropicrin is very toxic and should only be applied by contractors or approved operators.

(g)   D-D: D-D is a specific fumigant controlling eelworms. It is effective against club root (root knot eelworm) and potato root eelworm. This is slightly more effective than EDB but has to be applied early in the autumn to allow time for the dispersal of the fumes. The release of D-D, as with other fumigants, is dependant on soil type and temperature; in heavier soils with high organic content and low temperatures the release is slow and a time allowance should be made for these factors.

(h)   Ethylene Dibromide (EDB):   It is a specific fumigant that is active only against eelworms. It is used to control club root (root knot eelworm) against which it has proved effective. Its particular usefulness lies in the fact that it evaporates more readily and disperses at lower temperatures than some of the other soil fumigants. This enables its use later during autumn and on colder soils.

(i)   Nabam: Nabam is the chemical name of a product called Dithane

A40. This chemical is related to metham sodium but has different properties. It can be used as a soil sterilant some 2-3 weeks before planting. In a more dilute form it is applied regularly throughout the season as a fungicide. The soil sterilisation method is to work the soil thoroughly and soak the whole of the soil. This chemical is a specific contact fungicide useful against root rots.

(j) Methyl Bromide: This chemical shows great promise as a nematicide. It is very effective against club root (root knot eelworm) and evidence from elsewhere suggests that it has a fair degree of control over certain soil-borne fungal diseases as well as weeds.

Release of Chemicals

In the foregoing paragraphs the problems associated with the release of chemicals from the soil has been mentioned under specific chemicals. There are certain conditions that apply to chemical release that are of general application. Wet soils, and soils high in organic matter, will retain chemicals for longer than other soils. Care should be taken to dry wet soils, or to treat early in soils where there is a high water table, or allow a much longer period of time to elapse between treating and planting. Following application of chemicals some form of seal may be necessary; this can be either water or a layer of thin polythene. The time intervals, quoted by the manufacturers, from application to start of release should be adhered to. The actual release is normally easy, provided that the soil was in the correct condition to start with. This release is usually done by forking or spading and leaving the soil in a loose condition, with the ventilating lights open. In some soils rotary cultivation is all that is necessary. Finally it is important to remember that the times given by manufacturers for release of chemicals are average times. These may vary with soil type and condition, but it is unwise to allow less than the recommended time.

When using any of the chemicals mentioned above, care should be taken to read the manufacturers' recommendations and follow these as closely as possible. If protective clothing is recommended, then use it, to safeguard your own or an employee's health.

Special attention should be paid to the soil condition when sterilants are applied. The time the chemical is left in the soil before general release is very critical and should never be shortened. Finally, it is important that the chemical should have dispersed completely before plants are brought into the greenhouse.

Physiological Disorders

Peppers suffer from several physiological disorders which cause fruit to be downgraded or rejected. Fruit cracking has already been mentioned. Cracks around the shoulder of the fruit are generally symptoms of a widely fluctuating temperature regime, and possibly of humidity changes, especially early in the day. There is generally an increase in cracking after the heating has been turned off, especially if this is done early.

Sunburn, or scald, appears as a patch of necrotic grey tissue on the upper surface of the fruit. This is caused, as the name suggests, by the direct action of solar radiation on the fruit surface. It is a common problem in the summer, and can only be corrected by allowing the crop to develop a denser foliage or by shading the glasshouse.

Similar necrotic areas sometimes occur on the lower end of the fruit, and resemble 'black spot' of tomatoes. This type of fruit rot appears to be related to that tomato disorder, in that it is linked to root action and calcium uptake by the plant. It can therefore be corrected, or its effects minimised, by reducing the salt concentration if this is high, or increasing the watering rate if this is inadequate. These are the two factors which most commonly induce calcium deficiency symptoms, but in some cases a fungicide application may be necessary to improve root action, or even a direct increase in the calcium content of the substrate (such as by the addition of lime or Nitro-chalk) where analysis shows this to be low.

PART II: AUBERGINES

7:   Introduction; Propagation

The aubergine belongs to the same family — Solanaceae — as peppers, but is more closely related to the potato. There are a number of varieties in cultivation, both for edible and for ornamental use, and they are all forms of the species Solanum melongena.

Aubergines, also known as egg-plants or, in some Asian countries, brinjals, have been in cultivation for several centuries. Various breeding lines have developed, the main two originating in India and China respectively. Aubergines were introduced into Europe in the thirteenth century, at first into Italy, and eventually throughout the Mediterranean area.

The vast majority of aubergines produced are from outdoor field crops, but there has been an increasing interest in growing under protected cultivation in Europe, and a corresponding market premium for the better quality fruit produced in this way. The Netherlands, in particular, have developed a strong aubergine production area under glass, and experimental work and practical experience have kept pace with this development to provide up-to-date cultural information. Both Italy and France have considerable acreages of aubergines grown in the open, Italy alone producing over three hundred thousand tons annually.

In habit, the aubergine plant is quite similar to the pepper, although the leaves are much larger and more fleshy. The plant grows upright on a woody stem, but needs some form of support to prevent the stem from collapsing when carrying a weight of fruit. The plant tends to continue with a dominant growing point, unlike the pepper which divides into two more or less equivalent shoots at each flower level, but, like the tomato plant, has a particularly strong side-shoot at each fruiting level which can be used to subdivide the plant into further stems if needed. Side-shoots may form in the axils of all the leaves, but their further development will depend on the overall vegetative vigour of the plant, which in turn depends on the number of shoots already in active growth and on the fruit load. As will be described below, side-shoots are generally removed from leaf axils as soon as the desired plant form has been built up, although there are situations where late side-shoots near the base of the plant will be allowed to develop fruit in older crops.

Flowers form in levels up the stem of the aubergine in much the same way as with peppers. A single bloom may develop, or two or more, but one bloom is generally larger than the others, and this one alone is normally allowed to develop into a fruit, the others being removed during trimming. Flower setting, as will be described in more detail later, does not have to be associated with pollination. Fruit development is parthenocarpic, and quite often few or no seeds are found in the mature fruit. This is of no significance commercially, except of course in the case of crops grown for seed production.

Equipment

Since we are describing the culture of aubergines in protected cultivation, the first consideration must be for the structure itself. Like peppers and other vegetable crops, aubergines can be successfuly grown in a wide range of structures from polythene tunnels up to widespan alloy glasshouses. The limitations of any particular structure will depend on the climate and on the growing programme adopted. Aubergines are very light-dependent. The ability of any individual flower to develop a marketable fruit is related to the total light levels received by the plant and, apparently, also to the amount of light reaching the flower itself. Because of this, winter-started crops can generally only be grown successfully in structures with good light transmission.

Apart from light, the other climatic factors which need careful consideration are temperature and humidity. Aubergines will develop successfully only at quite high temperature levels, particularly during the early stages of growth (see below). Because of this aubergines grown without heat in Western Europe cannot be planted out before about the middle of April, leaving a very limited cropping season. Early crops must be heated and, because soil temperature is particularly important, the earliest crops should be planted only in houses with pipe heating, preferably with the additional facility of a soil warming system. Warm air heating units are suitable only for second-early crops, say planting in late March rather than from the middle of January onwards.

The control of humidity is important, because aubergines are even more susceptible to attack by botrytis than are peppers. Pipe heating systems are valuable in this respect, since a continuous input of low-level heat can be provided whenever damp conditions occur, so maintaining air movement through the crop and keeping it dry. Warm air heating is less satisfactory.

Adequate ventilation is essential for humidity control, and because of this the more basic form of polythene structure is unlikely to grow successful aubergine crops, particularly if it is unheated.

One further factor which must be kept in mind when planning to grow aubergines in any particular structure is the question of headroom.

Aubergines grown well will elongate rapidly. Unlike tomatoes, their stem is not supple enought to be bent into a training system, and so when the plant reaches the limit of its headroom it must be stopped. Subsequent re-growth from lower down the plant is possible, but slow, and leaves a long gap in production. One way to reduce this disadvantage in low houses is to use wider plant spacings, but to train up more stems per plant. This has the effect of slowing growth by increasing the fruit load on the plant, but will probably give a lower overall yield. Late and autumn plantings will not generally have this problem.

Apart from the structure and heating system, other equipment requirements must be considered. An irrigation system capable of delivering accurate and uniform water applications to the crop is necessary. This should also have the facility of applying liquid fertilisers, either directly from the storage tank or reservoir, or via a dilution or feed injection system. Overhead sprinklers are suitable for the early stages of growth, but may be less satisfactory later on when they can be obstructed by stems above the crop wires. Low-level spraylines are not suitable for the first few weeks until the lowest leaves are removed, but do a good job after this. Trickle and drip irrigation systems are suitable throughout the season, and are generally preferred for this reason.

Carbon dioxide enrichment is accepted as an economic cultural technique for aubergines, although there is no direct experimental evidence to confirm this. This enrichment can be provided in a number of ways, as described in detail in the pepper section — pure carbon dioxide, burning propane or paraffin, or using exhaust gases from suitable heating fuels. Control equipment should be provided for the heating system, and for the automatic ventilators if available, and thermostats should be housed in an aspirated screen. Temperature monitoring should be via integrating bottles, and soil and air screen thermometers (see peppers).

Soils and Fertilisers

Little work has been done in Western Europe on the soil and nutritional requirements of aubergines. Growth is generally more compact when crops are grown in heavy soils rather than on lighter substrates such as sandy soils. Because of this, it is possible that a rather higher level of base fertilisers should be used to limit vegetative growth in light soils. Aubergines have a stronger root system than peppers, and, like tomatoes, carry the potential risk of over-vegetative growth to the detriment of fruit production. It is therefore best to apply base fertilisers at approximately the same rates overall as for tomatoes, but with a little more emphasis on nitrogen supply.

Peat or organic fertilisers may be used to improve soil condition, but organic fertilisers should be limited to about one cubic metre per 100 square metres (1cm depth when spread) to avoid the risk of excessive salt or nutrient levels. Although vegetative growth continues better than is the case with peppers if the salt level is above normal, the crop will eventually become stunted, with dark foliage and reduced fruit size. In crops grown without the benefit of soil or pipe heating, it is possible to raise the level of the growing bed above the path by the addition of bulky soil conditioning materials such as straw or peat, and so encourage warmer soil conditions for the roots.

German work suggests that the soil pH for aubergines should be in the range 6.5 to 7.2 for optimum growth, and carbonate of lime should be used to raise the pH to this level if necessary. Aubergines appear to be particularly sensitive to magnesium deficiency, and so this should be incorporated into the soil as a base fertiliser. Magnesium limestone will increase the soil magnesium level and raise the pH at the same time.

Varieties

Until about 1973 the standard variety in Western Europe for protected cultivation was Mammouth, itself probably a selection from the older variety Long Purple. A number of varieties from several parts of the world, both from Indian and Chinese base stocks, were trialled in Holland at the Experimental Stations at Wageningen and Naaldwijk, but none of these matched the performance of Mammouth. However, it was already known at this time that a few established aubergine growers in the Netherlands had, by a process of selection, developed their own varieties, which were capable of yielding more and bigger fruit than Mammouth.

In the period 1973-5 these previously jealously-guarded selections were made available to Dutch commercial seed producers, and this led to the introduction of a new range of commercial varieties which immediately superceded Mammouth. Trials of these new varieties, among them Vedette, Claresse and Radja, showed them to produce up to half as many fruit again as Mammouth and for the fruit size also to be significantly greater. This meant that a grower could expect to double his yield simply by changing his variety, and this obviously put an entirely new perspective on the economics of aubergine production.

The wider availability of these selections is not the end of the story. These initially introduced new varieties are all quite similar, and are 'straight' varieties rather than hybrids. Since their release, commercial plant breeders have been working on a number of factors, including the production of F1 hybrids, to increase production, and to examine the potential of different fruit size and shape. Several markets prefer smaller rather than larger individual fruit, and so effects are being made to develop selections which yield a higher number of smaller fruit. There have also been attempts to evaluate the market acceptability of longer, thinner fruit or of globular fruit, although the intermediate shape of most current commercial varieties seems to be the most popular at the present time.

Seeds; Germination

There are usually about 180 aubergine seeds per gram (5,000 per ounce), but, because germination is often quite erratic and a proportion of the seedlings are not usable, it is better to assume that 100 plants (2,800 per ounce) will be produced. Seed can be sown in trays or in seedbeds, although because of the high temperature requirement for germination seedbed sowing is really only satisfactory if undersoil heating is available, or for summer sowings. The seed should be covered to a depth of about ½ cm and covered with glass to prevent damage by mice. A sowing density of only 1-2 grams per square metre is usual. This is because seedlings need to reach a comparatively large size before pricking off, so that abnormal plants can be discarded. Soaking the seed before sowing appears to give no advantage in speed or uniformity of germination, but it is possible to chit the seed in moist sand, and to prick off each seedling as the germination begins.

Although germination is very temperature-dependent, excessively high temperatures can also give problems, and a temperature regime between 19-26°C (67-78°F) is satisfactory. As soon as emergence is complete, this temperature can be allowed to fall a little. Pricking off into the propagation unit is usually delayed until the first true leaf is well visible, because a number of seedlings which show strap-like leaves with light flecks on them will need to be discarded at this stage.

Grafted Plants

It is possible to graft aubergine plants onto tomato rootstock, and so provide resistance to soil-borne problems such as wilts, corky root, brown root rot and root knot nematode. Trials carried out at Naaldwijk in Holland in 1974 used the tomato rootstock variety MM, which is resistant to both fusarium and verticillium wilts, grafting on to this aubergine plants of the variety Vedette.

The aubergine seeds need to be sown one to two weeks before the tomatoes, because of the longer time needed for germination and early growth, and the plants should be ready for grafting in about five weeks after sowing the rootstock under good growing conditions. The aim is to produce plants of roughly equal size and stem thickness. The thinner the stem, the more difficult is the grafting technique. The graft is made by making a diagonal cut in the tomato rootstock about 5cm above soil level and inserting a similar cut in the aubergine stem into this (see diagram),

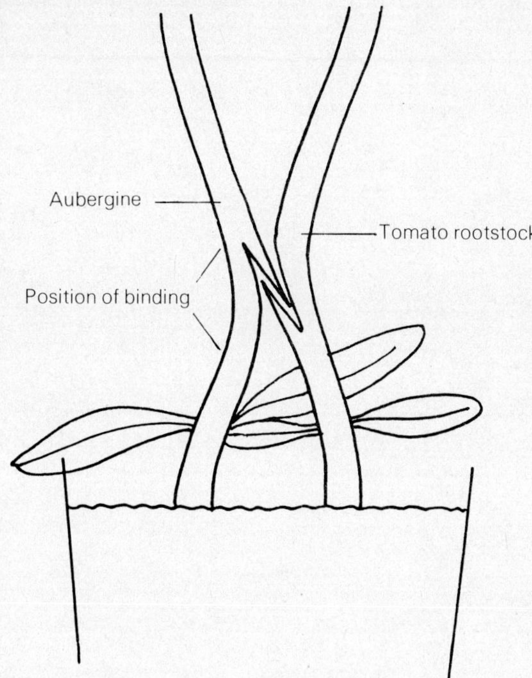

DIAGRAM 3.   Grafting plants in the pot.

binding the junction with a plastic tape or tin foil. The technique requires a very sharp knife, razor blade or scalpel, and a clean working surface to prevent the graft becoming contaminated with soil. The plants are then re-potted, in combination, and kept out of direct sunlight until well established.

After 2-3 weeks the aubergine plant is severed from its roots below the graft, and the grafted plant can then be planted out into its final position a few days later. Plant development should then be quite satisfactory, although a little chlorosis may be seen in the early stages. The yield potential and fruit quality would seem to match those from plants put out directly into well-sterilised ground.

Propagation

The size of the propagation pot will depend on the length of the propagation period, which in turn depends on the growing programme. An early sowing destined to be planted out in a pipe-heated structure will need a propagation period of nine to ten weeks. Later sowings, for warm-air heated houses, will grow more quickly in the better light conditions of early spring, and will reach planting stage in eight or nine weeks, while plants being raised through the summer months for autumn cropping may need as little as seven weeks. In all cases, the propagation period is longer than for tomatoes, and a good volume of compost is essential. Plastic or bituminised pots should generally be around 12-14cm diameter, while soil or peat blocks of 9-10cm size are commonly used. The starting nutrient levels in the compost should be the same as for tomatoes — extra nitrogen will be needed in the later stages of propagation, but this is best given by liquid feeding rather than in the initial base fertilisers.

After pricking off into the pots or blocks, these should be spaced with only a small gap between them, especially if they are on slatted or wire mesh benches, otherwise excessive drying out of the compost may occur. As the plants grow they can then be gradually spaced out to prevent the leaves from overlapping. A final spacing of 20cm square or even more may be needed. As with peppers, compost temperature is of great importance, and plants in pots with a good air circulation around them will develop much more rapidly than pots on solid benching or stood on the floor (unless underfloor heating is used).

Propagation temperatures should remain quite high to encourage a good growth rate. The night temperature should be in the range of 16-19°C (61-67°F), and the positive day temperature 19-22°C (61-71°F), running up to 27°C (80°F) in sun. The precise temperature regime will depend on the season, rather lower temperatures being used in the low light levels of January than for later sowings in better condtions. The higher temperatures are more suitable in the presence of carbon dioxide enrichment, and temperatures should be one or two degrees lower where this facility is not available. Carbon dioxide enrichment should be used as for tomatoes or peppers, giving a target level fo 1000ppm from dawn for an eight hour period, or until an hour before dusk in the period of shortest days. The precautions described for preventing damage to pepper plants by noxious by-products of combustion apply equally well to aubergines.

Lighting and Fuel Saving

Aubergines respond particularly well to supplementary lighting directly after emergence, and because of this it is possible to produce a larger plant more quickly at little expense. A single 400 watt mercury vapour lamp suspended a metre above a bench will illuminate about two square metres satisfactorily. Two such batches of seedlings can be illuminated on a twelve hour cycle, changing at midday and midnight (if practicable!), so providing a capacity of about 1,600 seedlings per two-week throughput from a single lamp.

For this purpose the seedlings should preferably be space-sown at about

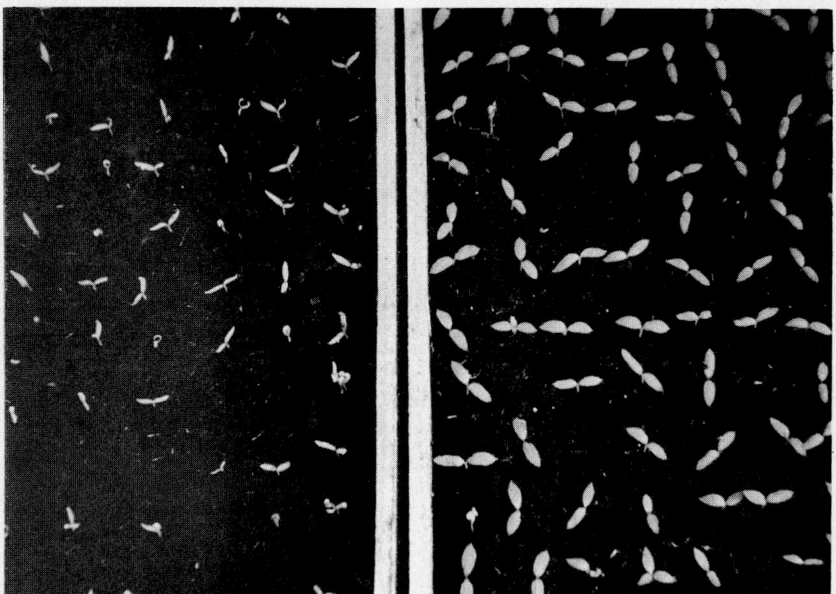

FIG 19. Aubergine seed is usually slow and erratic to germinate. This is characteristic of the seed, and even optimum cultural conditions can result in the range of seedling emergence shown here. The box on the right has received ten days supplementary lighting after emergence, showing the considerable improvement in rate of growth that this technique can provide. Note the variation in form of the seedlings.

400 per square metre and, ideally, chitted for maximum uniformity. The boxes directly under the lamp should occasionally be interchanged with those on the edges of the lit area to reduce the effect of variation in level of illumination, and also in local heating from the lamp.

Because of their long propagation period and slow growth rate in the early stages, aubergines provide the same opportunities for fuel saving as do peppers. They can be retained at a closer plant density beyond the normal standing-out time by planting them up at this stage into larger containers and holding them for a further period in this way. Economic and cultural aspects of this system are discussed in the section covering peppers, but it must be remember that aubergines develop larger leaves than peppers and so their space requirement will be greater at any particular time.

Again, because of the high temperature regimes needed for optimum growth of aubergines, the arguments in favour of thermal screens or forms of double glazing apply to this crop in the same way as to peppers, both for the propagation unit and for the growing-on-houses. The limitations in terms of both light transmission and humidity are equally applicable, too.

Watering and Feeding

According to the type of compost used and the rate of growth of the plants initial watering requirements can vary widely. The substrate should never be allowed to dry out completely, but neither should it remain permanently wet, as this would retard root action. In the later stages of propagation, when the plants have a considerable leaf area, the compost may dry very quickly in good growing conditions, and watering frequency will need to be high at this time. In addition to watering, the plants should be damped down occasionally in sunny weather to raise the humidity in the house and therefore to encourage active growth. This must be done with caution, particularly in the case of plants raised on the floor, on solid benching, or in boxes, as the foliage should always be dry by nightfull to discourage the spread of botrytis.

Because of the rather long propagation stage of aubergines, it is usual to apply liquid feed during the last few weeks, particularly to increase the available nitrogen in the compost. If the starting levels of nutrients in the substrate are according to normal tomato propagation requirements, liquid feed should be applied with every watering from about the firth or sixth week, according to the rate of growth. A suitable fertiliser would be a high nitrogen (1.0.1) feed (see appendix) diluted to give 250 ppm each of nitrate and potash. This feed should never be applied to very dry compost, and if the compost does dry excessively at any time then clear water should be applied initially to avoid the risk of root scorch. In poor growing conditions, and especially in waterlogged compost, the young plants may develop a yellow 'eye' characteristic of iron deficiency. This can be corrected by watering or spraying with a very weak iron chelate solution, but continued improvement in growth will only be maintained if the substrate condition improves to allow good root action.

Planting Out

When a suitable sized plant has been achieved — after seven to ten weeks of propagation according to the time of year — the plants should either be moved into the cropping house or potted on if an intermediate 'holding' stage at higher plant density is to be employed. The number and arrangement of plants will depend on the growing system to be employed. It is usual to grow aubergines in such a way that there are five to seven shoots per square metre of house, and a common way of achieving this is to plant three rows per 3.2 metre bay of a standard multi-span house, spacing the plants 60-75cm apart down the row, and training three or four shoots per plant. Some growers prefer to use only two rows per bay, with a correspondingly higher density of shoots in the row.

The more shoots that are trained up on a plant, then the slower they will

FIG 20. Aubergine seedlings ready for pricking off after a period of supplementary lighting. At this stage a proportion of seedlings will show strap-like distorted leaves, and these should be rejected.

grow, and the longer they will take to reach the crop wires. This can be an advantage in a long-season crop, even though the total weight of fruit may be a little reduced by the greater stress on the root system. Conversely, short-term crops, where shoot vigour should be kept to a maximum, may do better with a rather higher plant density but with only two shoots taken per plant. Autumn crops should have a lower shoot density than spring crops, since they are cropping under more adverse light and humidity conditions, and should be at a maximum of five shoots per square metre (three shoots per plant at 60cm plant spacing). In general, the greater the shoot density in the house within the range given above, then the greater the number of fruit produced, but the smaller the fruit size. This fruit size reduction under close planting conditions may have an economic advantage even if there is no overall yield gain, because there is often a market premium for low to middle sized fruit over the largest fruit.

Growing Systems

In general, the notes on aubergine culture which follow refer to crops grown in the soil. However, aubergines are also suitable for growing in soilless culture systems in the same way as tomatoes and peppers. Successful aubergine crops have already been produced in peat modules, in peat troughs and in rockwool, and there is no reason to believe they will not equally well adapt to nutrient film techniques. The information given on these various systems in the pepper section of this book applies equally well to aubergines, whose strong rooting habit gives them a good buffering capacity against minor cultural faults. Their sensitivity to temperature, particularly to root temperature, matches well the opportunity for substrate warming which is inherent in these various soilless growing systems.

8:   Growing On

As with peppers, the cropping success of aubergines depends to a large extent on good establishment into the growing-on house. Although aubergines are more inclined to make vegetative growth than peppers, and so a balance must be kept between plant vigour and fruit development in much the same way as the tomatoes, weakly rooting plants seldom recover well enough to yield a satisfactory crop.

The two factors which mainly control the speed of establishment are soil temperature and the physical state of the plant's root system. Poor root action will follow planting into soils which are cold or wet, and a mean temperature of at least 18°C (65°F) and preferably 20°C (68°F) should be the target. If a soil warming facility is not available, then the crop programme, from sowing date onwards, should be arranged according to anticipated soil temperatures at planting time. This point is discussed further under crop programmes. If the soil is colder than optimum at planting time, then one or two posibilities should be considered. The plants could be planted in large soil-filled pots or rings, which hold the rooting zone up above the soil. This allows the substrate temperature to come up to air temperature levels, or even higher in sun. Alternatively, the level of the soil in the planting trench itself can be raised by the addition of bulky soil conditioners, so allowing the sun's rays to warm up the substrate more effectively and assisting free drainage of the root zone. Whatever planting system is adopted, root temperatures can be improved by planting the propagation pot as shallow as possible, so that early rooting out is in the warmer soil layer close to the surface.

The other factor affecting early root establishment into the floor is the physical state of the root system, and this in turn is governed by the size of the plant in relation to the volume of compost, and by the care with which watering and feeding have been carried out during propagation. It has already been suggested that a large pot is necessary to allow normal root development during the long propagation stage, and during the later stages root scorch can quickly follow the application of liquid feeds on to dry compost. The aim should be to plant out a pot which is full of active white root, and not to delay beyond this stage, when the plant can soon become pot-bound.

Temperatures

The temperature requirements for aubergines after planting are generally quite similar to those for tomatoes. Rapid growth should be encouraged right from the start, and this in particular demands a soil temperature in the region of 20°C (68°F). Air temperatures should initially run at about 18-20°C (65-68°F) at night, and 21-22°C (70-73°F) by day. The higher temperatures in the range should be used if carbon dioxide enrichment is available or if light levels are good, and the lower temperatures for early crops growing in adverse conditions. Aubergines can take quite high temperatures in sunny weather, and a ventilation temperature of 27-28°C (80-82°F) should be set to take full advantage of this.

As soon as flowers appear, night temperatures should be lowered to encourage fruit development. This requires a good differential between day and night temperature, and so night heating should be cut down to run at about 17°C (63°F). To encourage the plants to continue active vegetative growth under a heavy fruit load it is advisable to reduce night temperatures still further as picking begings, say to 15°C (59°F). This brings a danger that the bulky fruit becomes cold during the night, and then a rapid air temperature increase in the morning causes condensation on the fruit surface, with a consequently greater risk of botrytis. To reduce this risk it may be necessary to maintain a little ventilation at all times, and to keep some warmth (say 40°C; 104°F) in the heating pipes to encourage air movement around the fruit.

Temperature requirements for autumn crops are basically the same as for long-season crops. In the early stages of growth, of course, there is no requirement for heating. However, as the duller and damper weather of the autumn approaches the problem of keeping the crop, and in particular the fruit, dry makes a pipe heating system essential. This should be used primarily for controlling humidity rather than temperature, but maintaining a minimum pipe heat of 40°C (104°F), and ventilating as necessary.

Fruit Development

Technically speaking, it is not entirely correct to refer to fruit setting in the case of aubergines, because the flowers are capable of developing into quite normal fruit without pollination or seed production. The fruit is properly referred to a parthenocarpic, and few seeds and generally found in mature aubergines unless they have been grown specifically for seed production. Once a flower has opened it may develop a fruit quickly, slowly, or not at all. The speed at which fruit development begins after the bloom opens is the main factor determining eventual fruit size at maturity, and so it is clearly important to know what encourages good 'setting'. There are two factors principally involved — flower strength and the temperature differential between day and night. There is no doubt that the larger the

FIG 21. Poor rooting conditions after planting can cause stunted growth and the yellow heads which are characteristic of reduced iron deficiency. In this case the peat substrate has become waterlogged.

FIG 22. Once the plant has established in the growing house and begins extensive growth, it can be trimmed down to the required number of strong shoots for subsequent tying—in this case, three.

flower is when it opens, then the quicker it begins to develop a fruit and so the greater is the fruit size at harvest. To encourage the production of large flowers it is necessary to consider mainly the balance between vegetative and fruit growth. If the plant is growing strongly, but under control, then the flower size will be good. If growth weakens, as will happen if the root action is impaired or if the plant is carrying a heavy burden of fruit under adverse climatic conditions, then flower size will be reduced and fruit development will slow or stop. This leads to a series of fruit 'flushes' and an uneven cropping pattern, and can only be improved by encouraging more plant vigour. How this is achieved will depend on the original problem — a fungicide root drench if the root action is poor, or perhaps more nitrogen in the feeding programme, or lower ventilation temperatures.

Poor flower development, and so poor 'setting', will also follow if the plant becomes over-vegetative. Aubergines generally have a strong rooting system, and in good growing conditions when the plant is carrying little fruit, shoot growth can become too strong and flower size will drop. To correct this may call for a reduction in watering or an increased feed strength, or perhaps higher day temperatures. There is a strong correlation between rate of development of flowers into fruit and the differential between day and night temperatures. A difference of, say 5°C or more between mean day and night temperatures encourages rapid fruit development, while setting may fail completely if night temperatures run as high as day temperatures. This in turn leads to increased plant vigour as the fruit load on the plant reduces, and so the situation worsens as flower size drops.

At each flower level on the plant there are often produced one main bloom and one or more secondary blooms. The smaller blooms may be attached directly to the stem of the plant, or form a 'spray' with a common stalk. These secondary blooms are invariably smaller than the main flower, and set only slowly, if at all, to produce small fruit which may or may not be marketable. It is common commercial practice to remove these secondary flowers during the trimming operation to reduce this less acceptable fruit load on the plant, and so maintain vegetative growth. Whether this operation is economically sound will depend on the overall vigour of the crop.

Some work has been carried out on hormones and related materials as an aid to fruit development. These are mainly applicable to field crops, and should not be considered a substitute to good culture.

Watering and Feeding

The water requirements of an aubergine crop will vary widely according to its vigour and stage of growth and also according to the soil type, to climatic factors and to the growing system used. It is therefore quite impossible to give any hard and fast rules about either quantity or frequency of watering. If in doubt, common sense is the best policy — the rooting zone should never be excessively dry, but neither should it be continually at field capacity. If plant vigour is excessive, then the watering rate can be reduced a little, as it can if growth is stunted, since the plant will be calling for less water if it is not in good active growth.

If the crop is being grown in a peat or rockwool substrate, then liquid feeding should begin at planting time and continue with every watering unless substrate analysis shows that nutrient levels have risen excessively. With soil grown crops it is usual to begin feeding after three or four weeks, when the roots are well established. Because aubergines are a leafy crop, and because it is generally necessary to encourage vigour once fruit development is well under way, the most commonly used liquid feed is based on the medium nitrogen feed (1.0.1). The formulae for this and other feeds are given in an appendix. If crop vigour becomes excessive, then a temporary change to a feed with more potash (e.g. 1.0.2) may be required, together with an increase in feed strength. Conversely, if shoot development becomes very poor, then extra vigour may be encouraged by using a high nitrogen (2.0.1) feed for a short period.

Aubergines appear to be rather insensitive to phosphate levels, perhaps because of their extensive root system, and so it will not usually be necessary to incorporate phosphate into the feeding programme for soil grown crops, although this will be needed for peat or other soilless substrates. However, aubergines seem to suffer very readily from magnesium deficiency, and so it would be wise to include this reguarly in the liquid feed, using magnesium sulphate according to the formula given in the appendix. Where root action has been reduced by poor soil conditions such as waterlogging or low temperatures, or by root scorch, then trace element deficiencies may affect the crop, notably iron, and the addition of low levels of chelated trace elements may then be incorporated in the feed to counteract this.

General Culture

It has already been said that carbon dioxide enrichment is of value during the propagation stage. This is equally true after planting, and enrichment at 1000ppm during the daytime until the ventilators are continually open will repay any additional cost in terms of both earliness and total yield. Ventilation temperatures can be a little higher if carbon dioxide enrichment is being used than if it is not.

Because aubergines are so sensitive to botrytis infection, then overhead sprays to encourage better growth in sunny conditions must be applied with caution. Unlike tomatoes, aubergines do not rely directly on humidity changes for fruit setting, and so regular sprays are less important. The primary site for botrytis is generally the surface of the developing fruit beneath the calyx, particularly if the petal-ring remains attached, as this is spongy and holds water for some time. Despite this, overhead sprays in sunny weather should be applied occasionally to reduce excessive leaf temperature and to raise humidity, provided it is always possible to have the crop dry by nightfall.

Crop Management

Aubergine plants should be tied around the main stem when they reach a height of about 30cm, using a plastic string and ensuring that the loop around the plant is loose enough to allow normal stem thickening without cutting in. Alternatively, the first string can be placed under the pot at planting time, the extensive root system of the plant soon anchoring it in place. Once the crown flower has formed, the first strong sideshoots develop, and these should be retained as needed, being themselves tied up to the crop wires as soon as they begin to elongate. It may also be worthwhile to run horizontal strings above each row to hold in the developing shoots and to keep the paths clear.

Once the required number of leading shoots have been tied, remaining sideshoots should be removed down to the base of the plant. Removing shoots should then be a routine weekly operation, together with twisting the developing stems around their strings. At the same time one or two small leaves close to the head of each stem should be removed to reduce later foliage density. Other jobs which can be carried out during the weekly trimming include pinching off secondary flowers which are not needed for fruit production, and pulling off the petal-ring from fruit which are set to reduce the risk of botrytis becoming established.

Deleafing should begin three or four weeks after planting, and should then be carried out about every two weeks, the aim being to reduce foliage density so that light transmission to the developing flowers is sufficient, and also to expose fruit to make harvesting easier. A general reduction in foliage also reduces the risk of botrytis infection developing by encouraging drying air movement through the crop. This is particularly important in the case of autumn crops, which often have to cope with humid conditions. When deleafing is carried out, any secondary sideshoots which have developed low down on the plants should be removed, except that when the plant has grown well up towards the crop wire and the bottom of the stems are clear, some of these late developing shoots can be left to develop fruit which are usually rather small, but of marketable quality.

Harvesting

Like green peppers, the stage at which an aubergine fruit should be harvested can be difficult to identify at first. The fruit is initially very dark purple when immature, and when it is fully ripe it is a very pale colour. In between these two conditions is the harvesting stage. The fruit begins to lighten from the tip of the fruit, and this paling of the colour gradually extends back towards the calyx. The fruit should be harvested when this lightening is first seen, although it can be left on the plant for up to a week after this without loss of quality. Aubergines left beyond this time become pale and unattractive, while prematurely picked fruit quickly wrinkle and soften, and have a much reduced shelf-life.

Picking is usually carried out weekly, although it is possible to extend the picking interval to two weeks provided no fruit are missed. The fruit is cut from the plant with a knife or secateurs, retaining a section of the stalk on the fruit. Picking is quite a time-consuming operation, as care must be taken that the spines on the calyx do not damage the surface of adjacent fruit.

Sorting and Packing

Aubergines are usually graded by weight, a typical series of grades running as follows: —

> 100-175 grams
> 175-225   ,,
> 225-300   ,,
> 300-400   ,,
> 400-500   ,,
> over 500   ,,

The middle grade, say 225-400 grams, is the most acceptable size, and usually fetches a market premium. Grading by size in the packing shed can be carried out by hand, although larger aubergine producers frequently adapt cucumber grading machines for this purpose.

In addition to size grading, there should also be a form of quality grading, as with peppers, so that fruit which has blemishes caused by physical damage, cultural problems, pests or diseases can be marketed in a lower grade than top quality fruit. Fruit shape may also need to be taken into account, although this is usually quite uniform in a well-grown crop of a good variety.

Fruit must be handled with care at all stages, because of the risk of superficial damage by the spines on the calyces, and it is often necessary to polish or wash off any dirt or chemical residues to give an attractive appearance to the fruit. Because of this, the labour input for sorting and

FIG 23. Aubergine plants should be trimmed down and tied as soon as they can conveniently be handled. In this instance, a wide plant spacing has been adopted, and five shoots will be trained up from each plant. Closer planting, but with less shoots per plant, is more suitable in some situations.

FIG 24. Unwanted sideshoots should be removed regularly, otherwise the plant quickly becomes bushy, and crop management then becomes more difficult. Poorer light transmission to the lower part of the plant reduces fruit development, too.

packing aubergines can be high. Fruit is generally packed in 5kg boxes, which should have enough room to avoid damage in transit, although fruit destined for local sales may be presented in open trays or boxes if the market accepts this.

Fruit Storage

Aubergine fruit can be stored for up to two or three weeks at a temperature of 12-15°C (54-59°F), provided it has been picked mature, although the effect of such storage on subsequent shelf-life and quality has not been investigated. The humidity needs to be kept to about 80% to avoid excessive water loss from the fruit, but should not rise above this level because of the risk of botrytis. For the same reason, storage temperatures below 5-6°C (41-43°F) should be avoided.

Fruit cropped in the summer should be picked and left in the packing shed in preference to remaining on the plant. Temperatures regularly above 20°C (68°F) in the growing house can cause fruit deterioration, while it is usually possible to keep packing shed temperature rather below this.

FIG 25. The calyx of aubergine fruit is hard and spiky, and care should be taken in handling both the plant and the picked fruit to avoid damaging the fruit surface by abrasion of adjacent calyces.

FIG 26. Aubergine crops should be well leafed out to facilitate harvesting. This is even more important in the case of autumn crops, where high humidities quickly lead to fruit rotting if air circulation is poor.

FIG 27.. Aubergine fruit is bulky, and picking a large production area requires some sort of mechanical assistance to cut down the labour input. Small containers are less likely to result in fruit damage than bulk bins.

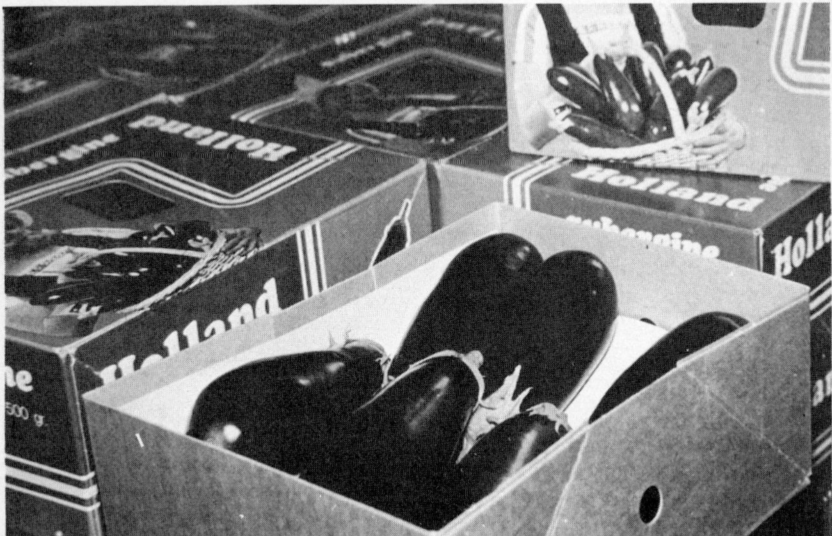

FIG 28. As with poppers, aubergines need to be packed for export in strong containers with plenty of room to accommodate the specified weight of fruit. Presentation is of considerable importance, if market value is to be maximised.

9: Programmes; Pests and Diseases

Cropping programmes for aubergines can be divided into three groups — early heated crops, cold summer crops, and heated autumn crops. Each of these groups has its particular requirements in terms of equipment, crop timing, and culture.

Early heated crops can be further subdivided into the earliest crops, for which a piped heating system is a necessity and undersoil heating an advantage, and second early crops for which warm air heating systems are adequate. The earliest heated crops should be sown at the beginning of December, and are ready for planting out from the middle of January to the beginning of February. For these crops, in addition to a heating system capable of providing suitable soil temperatures, it is necessary to have good quality glass with high light transmission, and plenty of head-room for the long season crop. Cultural standards need to be high to sustain a long crop and a good control of the glasshouse environment is necessary. If these conditions are met, then a yield of 40 fruits per square metre, each weighing 300-350 grams, is a realistic target, and crops of double this weight have been achieved.

Second early crops, suitable for structures in which the required soil temperature may be more difficult to achieve, are generally planted out during the second half of March, having been sown during late January. The success of these crops depends largely on weather conditions after planting, as the amount of direct sun heat reaching the soil will determine the speed of plant establishment and early growth. This is even more true of crops grown cold. Cold crops should not be planted out before the middle of April and are always a gamble. Fruit development is slow, and there are often serious problems with botrytis, both on the fruit and on the stem. For this reason unheated structures used for aubergines should be well ventilated and not subject to humidity problems. Polythene tunnels, especially less expensive types with poor ventilation, are not suitable.

Autumn crops are quite commonly grown, but to be worthwhile they should be planted at least by the middle of July, otherwise the cropping period is not long enough to achieve the minimum target yield of 10-12 fruit per square metre. This means that they cannot follow a previous aubergine crop, because the cropping period of the first crop would then be too short for it to be economic. A large plant should be used to make the most of the good summer growing conditions and so to come into production with as little delay as possible. Autumn crops are particularly susceptible to botrytis losses, and should therefore only be grown in houses with a pipe heating system which can be used to control humidity. The shoot density needs to be lower than for early crops to reduce this problem, and to encourage better fruit development as light levels fall in the autumn. A plant spacing of 60-70cm in the row is commonly used, with three rather than four stems being taken.

Crop Costings

The costs of production vary widely with the growing system and programme employed, and so standard costs cannot be quoted. In general, a comparison with tomato growing costs is useful, since these are generally known in some detail in most growing areas. Plant raising costs and most sundries will be quite similar to tomatoes, except for the greater fuel requirement, which can add fifty percent onto propagation fuel costs (see peppers). Pest and disease control costs will probably be higher than for tomatoes, since effective control of many problems requires aerosol or smoke applications rather than wet sprays.

The greatest differences in costings between tomatoes and aubergines occur in the labour and fuel sections. Heating costs are outlined in the pepper section and are always higher than for tomatoes for any particular growing programme, because of the higher temperature regime and also because of the fuel which must be used to provide humidity control. Labour requirements cannot be tabulated with precision, because they will vary according to the method of culture adopted, but it can be assumed that they are overall very similar to those for tomatoes. Trimming and deleafing labour will depend on the number of stems per unit area. Since there is a correlation between stem density and total yield, then the number of stems per square metre will depend on an economic balance between labour input and crop returns, with cultural factors further complicating the issue — higher densities will give smaller fruit, which may be more acceptable to the market, but add to the difficulty of pest and disease control. .

Although picking aubergines is a quick operation, this labour advantage over tomatoes is offset by the greater care needed in handling the fruit if mechanical damage is to be avoided, and by the need to clean the fruit in some situations. Labour input in the packing shed can be considerably reduced on larger production units by the use of mechanical handling and sorting equipment developed for cucumbers

Pest and Disease Control

Generally speaking, the pests and diseases which affect aubergines are also those which affect peppers, the principal exceptions being verticillium wilt and virus. Because of this, only brief notes will be given in this chapter, and readers are referred to the corresponding section under peppers for more detailed information on the symptoms and control measures.

As with peppers, an overall high standard of culture and hygiene are the most important factors in avoiding pests and diseases, together with crop management time devoted to the early identification of problems, and so applying suitable control measures, either cultural or chemical, before the situation gets out of hand. Smoke and fog applications of chemicals are generally better than high volume wet sprays, because of the greater crop penetration, but this is not as important as with peppers, especially if the crop is kept well trimmed and open.

Red Spider Mite

This is a common pest of aubergines, thriving on the high temperature regime employed for this crop, particularly in the low humidity conditions which are maintained to reduce botrytis problems. Biological control has been successfully used on red spider mite on aubergines, using the predator Phytoseiulus persimilis, or alternatively any of the range of acaricides recommended for peppers can be tried. However, grower experience with some of these chemicals is limited in the case of aubergines, and it would be wise to apply any acaricide to a small area intially to test for any phytotoxic effects.

Whitefly

The symptoms produced by this ubiquetous pest are much the same as for peppers, as is the range of chemicals used for its control. Biological control works well in both aubergine and pepper crops, probably because at the high temperatures employed the parasite is able to develop quickly and so maintain a good level of control over the whitefly. The parasite used is a small wasp, Encarsia formosa, and this is introduced into the crop in its pupal form, which consists of modified larval scales of its whitefly host. These are distinguished from unparasitised scales by being black rather than white or translucent.

Black scales should be introduced into the crop as soon as any adult whiteflies are seen, or even before this. It is usual to inoculate at the rate of 2-6 black scales per plant per introduction, and to make successive introductions at two-week intervals until parasitised whitefly scales visible on the lower surfaces of the aubergine leaves indicate that satisfactory establishment has occurred. From then onward, a number of factors have to be considered if a successful balance is to be maintained. Sideshoots should be removed on a regular and frequent basis. Old leaves should, however, be retained in the house for longer than normal to allow the black scale stage of the parasite to complete its life cycle and hatch into the adult wasp.

Chemical applications for other pests or diseases should be used only with caution, as many insecticides and fungicides are toxic to Encarsia. If in doubt, the supplier of the parasite should be able to offer advice on the suitability of particular chemicals. It is worthwhile using the red spider mite predator in conjunction with Encarsia, so that the risk of having to use an acaricide is reduced.

Aphids

As with peppers, greenfly attacks are common, but easily controlled. The same range of chemicals available for peppers is suitable for aubergines (including pirimicarb, dichlorvos, mevinphos and propoxur). Aubergines do not appear to suffer from any identifiable virus diseases, and so aphid control is not so urgent in this respect, but they can still cause considerable crop damage quickly in their own right, and so control measures should not be delayed once an outbreak is noticed. There is a parasitic wasp, Aphidius, which attacks greenfly, and can be identified by the gold-coloured 'mummified' case in which it develops. This often becomes established naturally in a crop without deliberate introduction, but its ability to maintain aphid populations to within acceptable limits is uncertain at the present time, and so its commercial use in a programme of integrated pest control is in some doubt.

Other Pests

Thrips occasionally infest aubergine crops, causing silvery flecks on the leaves and calyx. The range of chemicals available for aphids are generally suitable for control of thrips. Other pests occasionally found on aubergines are listed in the section dealing with pest control on peppers — caterpillars, leaf miner, eelworm and millipedes, for example.

Verticillium Wilt

This is a serious disease problem in aubergines, as it is soil-transmitted, and causes infected plants to die. The lower leaves wilt and turn yellow, often on one side of the central vein initially, and the disease gradually spreads upwards towards the growing point, generally working up one side of the plant. If the stem is cut through with a knife, the conducting tissue is usually stained brown on the side of the plant which is wilting. It is this development of the fungus in the vascular tissue which blocks water transport in the plant and causes the visible symptoms of the disease. This is the same disease which affects tomatoes, cucumbers and chrysanthemums. Chemical control measures appear to have little effect, although benomyl-type fungicides may reduce the spread of the disease. Infected plants should be removed, complete with the root system, as soon as the symptoms are observed. Extensive infection can be to some extent alleviated by shading the house and damping over the crop regularly in sunny weather to reduce physiological stress.

Botrytis

Botrytis is an ever-present danger in aubergine crops, as it is in peppers. Perhaps more so, because one of the primary sites of infection in aubergines is the fruit itself. Botrytis fruit rot quickly develops wherever humid conditions persist, and the fruit which is affected with the wet, brown lesions immediately becomes unmarketable. The development of botrytis lesions on the fruit often follows when the petal ring, which shrinks as the fruit starts to enlarge, becomes trapped between the small fruit and the calyx. This petal ring is rather spongy and absorbent, and holds water against the surface of the fruit, in which botrytis can become established. Once a lesion develops in this position on the fruit, the attachment to the calyx weakens and the fruit will then fall to the floor. This problem can be greatly reduced if removal of the petal ring after fruit development has started is included as a routine operation in crop management.

Botrytis can also infect stems and leaves as described for peppers, and control measures — both cultural and chemical — should follow those described for that crop.

Sclerotinia

Stem rot caused by the fungus sclerotinia can be identified on aubergines by a circling lesion, brown in colour, and often covered with small darker granules, which can eventually cause the death of the shoot. The lesion occasionally develops a white surface when conditions are moist, but generally lacks the grey fur characteristic of botrytis. This fungus is similar to botrytis in that it spreads most rapidly in warm humid conditions, and so control measures should follow the same pattern as for botrytis, aiming to reduce atmospheric humidity as far as practicable. Chemical control should also be as for botrytis. Sclerotinia can also infect the fruit, and all infected material should be removed from the house, rather than left on the floor, to reduce the spread of the disease.

Other Diseases

Good balanced growth in an aubergine crop is dependent on an active, healthy root system. A number of fungi can cause root rots, and should be avoided if possible. Good soil sterilisation should be adequate to prevent serious infection, but secondary attacks may follow physical root damage caused by chemical scorches, drying out, etc. If this occurs, a root drench of a suitable fungicide — zineb, or a copper-based material — should be given to clean up the roots and so recover root action.

Problems with virus infection of aubergine crops have not occurred in glasshouse culture up to the present, and so it is probable that the stocks used to develop modern varieties have considerable natural resistance to the common plant viruses which attack tomatoes, cucumbers and peppers.

Appendix 1:   Liquid Feeding

Preparation of Liquid Fertiliser Stock Solutions

(a) *Materials:* All liquid feeds are prepared from soluble fertiliser materials having the following or similar analyses: —

Potassium Nitrate	13% N, 45% K_2O
Ammonium Nitrate	35% N
Urea	46% N
Mono Ammonium Phosphate	11% N, 48% P_2O_5
Calcium Nitrate	15.5% N, 30% CaO
Magnesium Sulphate	16% MgO

These fertilisers should be of high quality grade materials and free of impurities and insoluble fractions.

Kieserite is not a suitable material for use as a liquid fertiliser.

(b) *Storage:*   All materials in the solid state should be stored in a dry, well ventilated shed or store room preferably in air tight containers such as a polythene bag.

(c) *Dissolving and Storage of Stock Solutions:*   The fertiliser mixtures listed below dissolve in cold water provided they are weighed out correctly and added to the appropriate quantity of water. Complete and even mixing is effected by suspending the solid fertiliser in the water and allowing it to percolate through a suitable open-weave material e.g. terylene gauze. Tipping the mixture directly into the tank may cause layering of a more concentrated solution at the bottom, even after thorough stirring. Hot or warm water will speed up the process and should be used whenever possible. The prepared stock solution should be prevented from becoming very cold as this causes the fertiliser salts to crystalise in the tank and in the pipe lines. However, the chemicals will redissolve satisfactorily when the temperature rises. Stock solutions can be stored satisfactorily provided the container is not zinc coated.

(d) *Colouring:* A dye may be added to the stock solution for convenience in use. Suitable materials are Disulphine blue at 50 grams in 40 gallons, or Caramel at 2 litres in 40 gallons of stock solution. Propietary dyes are available and should be used according to instructions. A point to note with colour dye is that wide variations in solution concentrations can occur with little or no visual differences in colour — they do not provide a reliable indication of the dilution rate.

(e) *Trace Elements:* On occasions the addition of trace elements are made to the fertiliser stock solution to provide copper, boron, iron, manganese, zinc and molybdenum to plants growing in soilless rooting media. These may be applied singly or as a mixture. Proprietary brands of trace element mixtures are available usually as chelated salts and should be applied according to the manufacturers recommendations. It is important not to exceed the recommended rates.

Calculating the Strength (PPM) of Proprietary Liquid Fertilisers

Concentrations of liquid fertilisers are usually given as percentages weight to volume (%W/V) or less frequently, as a percentage weight to weight (%W/W). From these figures the parts per million concentrations (ppm) or the dilution of any proprietary feed can be calculated as follows: —

Formulae:
(a)   For calculating nutrient concentration (ppm) in dilute feeds when the analysis of stock solution is expressed as %w/v:

$$\text{ppm in dilute solution} = \frac{\% \text{ w/v} \times 10{,}000}{\text{dilution}}$$

e.g. using fertiliser containing 4% N and 8% K_2O (w/v) at a dilution of

$$1{:}200 \text{ ppm N} = \frac{4 \times 10{,}000}{200} = \frac{400}{2} = 200 \text{ ppm N}$$

$$\text{ppm } K_2O = \frac{8 \times 10{,}000}{200} = \frac{800}{2} = 400 \text{ ppm } K_2O$$

(b)   For calculating nutrient concentration ppm in dilute foods when the analysis of stock solution is expressed as % w/w:

$$\text{ppm in dilute solution} = \frac{\% \text{ w/w} \times 10{,}000 \times 1.2}{\text{dilution}}$$

e.g. using a fertiliser containing 4% N and 8% K_2O w/w at a dilution of

$$1{:}200 \text{ ppm N} = \frac{4 \times 10{,}000 \times 1.2}{200} = \frac{400 \times 1.2}{2} = 240 \text{ ppm N}$$

$$\text{ppm } K_2O = \frac{8 \times 10{,}000 \times 1.2}{200} = \frac{800 \times 1.2}{2} = 480 \text{ ppm } K_2O$$

The introduction of the factor 1.2 in the formula takes into account the specific gravity of the stock solution.

(c)   For calculating the dilution necessary to give a particular concentration (ppm): — Dilution = $\dfrac{\% \text{ w/v} \times 10{,}000}{\text{ppm required}}$

e.g. using a stock solution containing 8% w/v K_2O and requiring 350 ppm K_2O in the diluted feed: —

$$\text{Dilution required} = \frac{8 \times 10,000}{350}$$

Therefore apply at a dilution of 1 in 228

Application of Liquid Fertilisers for Peppers and Aubergines

This section outlines the use of liquid fertiliser mixtures for these glasshouse crops.

Standard Liquid Fertilisers

Three standard liquid feeds are recommended for these crops covering normal requirements. These feeds are based on potassium nitrate to which may be added urea or ammonium nitrate in order to adjust the ratio of Nitrogen (N) to Potash (K_2O) as required by the crop. Magnesium sulphate may also be added to these feeds at the rates indicated.

Liquid Fertilisers containing Phosphate

Liquid fertilisers containing phosphate are often recommended for peppers and aubergines grown in soilless substrates. Mono-ammonium phosphate is then added to the standard feeds but OMITTING the magnesium sulphate.

Liquid Fertilisers containing Calcium

These feeds may be required in certain circumstances and are prepared by using calcium nitrate in the standard feeds. Both magnesium sulphate and mono-ammonium phosphate must be omitted from the feeds containing calcium nitrate and all storage vessels and lines should be flushed out before and after use.

Growers should note that they must not mix a liquid fertiliser containing phosphate with a feed containing calcium as this leads to the formation of insoluble calcium phosphate which, apart from making both the phosphate and the calcium unavailable to the plants, would result in blocking of nozzles and lines of the irrigation system. Magnesium sulphate is also omitted from both phosphatic and calcium feeds for similar reasons.

Standard Liquid Fertilisers (Using Urea)

All to be diluted at 1 in 200, or added directly to 200 gallons of water.

Feed	Feed Ratio $NP_2O_5.K_2O$	ppm K_2O in dilute feed	Fertilisers	Weight in grams per gallon of stock
Medium potash	1.0.2	350ppm	Potassium nitrate Urea	680gms 170gms
Medium nitrogen	1.0.1	250ppm	Potassium nitrate Urea	510gms 340gms
High nitrogen	2.0.1	125ppm	Potassium nitrate Urea	280gms 430gms

Standard Liquid Fertilisers (Using Ammonium Nitrate)

Feed	Feed Ratio $NP_2O_5.K_2O$	ppm K_2O in dilute feed	Fertilisers	Weight in grams per gallon of stock
Medium potash	1.0.2	350ppm	Potassium nitrate Ammonium nitrate	680gms 200gms
Medium nitrogen	1.0.1	250ppm	Potassium nitrate Ammonium nitrate	510gms 450gms
High nitrogen	2.0.1	125ppm	Potassium nitrate Ammonium nitrate	280gms 570gms

Magnesium sulphate may be added to any of the above feeds at the rate of 150-200gms per gallon.

Liquid Fertilisers containing Phosphate (Using Urea)

Feed	Feed Ratio $NP_2O_5.K_2O$	ppm K_2O in dilute feed	Fertilisers	Weight in grams per gallon of stock
Medium potash	1.1.2	350ppm	Potassium nitrate Mono-amm. phosphate Urea	680gms 340gms 85gms
Medium nitrogen	1.1.1	250ppm	Potassium nitrate Mono-amm. phosphate Urea 230g	510gms 450gms 230gms
High nitrogen	2.1.1	125ppm	Potassium nitrate Mono-amm. phosphate Urea	280gms 450gms 370gms

Phosphate Fertilisers using Ammonium Nitrate

Use the above table, but replace the urea with 1¼ times the weight of ammonium nitrate.

Calcium Fertilisers

Use the appropriate standard liquid fertiliser formula, but add 280 grams calcium nitrate per gallon of stock, and reduce the nitrate source (ammonium nitrate or urea) by 120 grams. This provides 100 ppm of calcium (as CaO) in the dilute feed.

Appendix 2:   Carbon Dioxide Consumption Estimates (Per Acre)

	Paraffin (galls)	Propane (kg)	Carbon Dioxide (kg)
January	520	1,950	5,850
February	540	2,020	6,060
March	590	2,230	6,690
April	510	1,620	4,860
May	520	1,670·	5,010
TOTAL	2,680 gallons	9,490kg	28,470kg

These figures are based on the assumption that enrichment begins at dawn, and switches off when the air temperature controls call for the ventilators to open, or an hour before dusk on dull days (up to a maximum of eight hours).

The estimates assume a Guernsey crop, planted out early in January, and enriched to 1,000ppm of carbon dioxide.

Appendix 3:   Useful Information

Calculations

Volume of a circular tank

Multiply half the circumference (in feet) by half the diameter (in feet) by the depth (in feet). Multiply the answer by 6.25 to give the capacity in gallons.

e.g. A tank with diameter 10ft, depth 8ft, and circumference 31.4ft.

$$\frac{31.4}{2} \times \frac{10}{2} \times 8 \times 6.25 = 3,920 \text{ gallons}$$

Conversion Factors

°C	°F
0	32
2	36
5	41
10	50
13	55
15	59
17	63
20	68
25	77
30	86

To convert		
From	*to*	*multiply by*
Inches	Centimetres	2.54
Centimetres	Inches	0.39
Metres	Feet	3.28
Sq. feet	Sq metres	0.093
Sq metres	Sq feet	10.76
Sq metres	Sq yards	1.20
Cubic metres	Cubic yards	1.31
Fluid oz.	Millilitres (cc)	28.4
Pints	Litres	0.57
Litres	Gallons	0.22
Ounces	Grams	28.4
Grams	Ounces	0.035
Pounds	Kilograms	0.45

Glasshouse volume (single span)

Add height to ridge (in feet) to height to eaves. Divide by two, and multiply by the width (in feet) and again by the length (in feet). This gives the volume in cubic feet.

e.g. Height to ridge 12 ft. Height to eaves 6 ft.
    Length 150ft. width 30ft.

$$\frac{12 + 6}{2} = 9 \times 150 \times 30 = 40,500 \text{ cubic feet.}$$

Appendix 4:   Peat Substrates

Growers wishing to manufacture their own peat modules, or mix a peat substrate for filling troughs or pots, should work to the following formula.
    To each bale (12 cubic feet) of medium grade sphagnum moss peat, add:

1.8kg	(4 lbs)	Magnesian limestone
150gms	(5 ¼ oz)	Ureaformaldehyde
300gms	(10 ½ oz)	Potassium nitrate
150gms	(5 ¼ oz)	Potassium sulphate
600gms	(21 oz)	Superphosphate
150gms	(5 ¼ oz)	Fritted trace elements

These materials, excluding the lime, can be pre-mixed, and then added at 1.35kg (3lbs) per 12 cubic feet of peat.